Blockchain:

Uncovering Blockchain Technology, Cryptocurrencies, Bitcoin and the Future of Money

Alan Wright

© 2017

COPYRIGHT

Blockchain: Learn Uncovering Blockchain Technology, Cryptocurrencies, Bitcoin and the Future of Money

By Alan Wright

Copyright @2017 By Alan Wright

All Rights Reserved.

The following eBook is reproduced below with the goal of providing information that is as accurate and as reliable as possible. Regardless, purchasing this eBook can be seen as consent to the fact that both the publisher and the author of this book are in no way experts on the topics discussed within, and that any recommendations or suggestions made herein are for entertainment purposes only. Professionals should be consulted as needed before undertaking any of the action endorsed herein.

This declaration is deemed fair and valid by both the American Bar Association and the Committee of

Publishers Association and is legally binding throughout the United States.

Furthermore, the transmission, duplication or reproduction of any of the following work, including precise information, will be considered an illegal act, irrespective whether it is done electronically or in print. The legality extends to creating a secondary or tertiary copy of the work or a recorded copy and is only allowed with express written consent of the Publisher. All additional rights are reserved.

The information in the following pages is broadly considered to be a truthful and accurate account of facts, and as such any inattention, use or misuse of the information in question by the reader will render any resulting actions solely under their purview. There are no scenarios in which the publisher or the original author of this work can be in any fashion deemed liable for any hardship or damages that may befall them after undertaking information described herein.

Additionally, the information found on the following pages is intended for informational purposes only and should thus be considered, universal. As befitting its nature, the information presented is without assurance regarding its continued validity or interim quality. Trademarks that mentioned are done without written consent and can in no way be considered an endorsement from the trademark holder.

How much is it worth?..67

How can I spend it?...67

Chapter 7: 70

Bitcoin Mastery 70

Preparation 70

What is a wallet? 71

What do you need to know about having a bitcoin wallet on your computer? 72

Getting Your First Bitcoins 77

Congratulations! You have just entered the bitcoin economy. 79

Buying Bitcoin Hand-to-Hand............................80

A couple of things to note: 80

Where can you buy bitcoin like this?..................82

How Not to Buy Bitcoin....................................86

Chapter 8: 88

Bitcoin mining 88

What is Bitcoin mining?......................................89

Technical Background..90

Bitcoin Mining Hardware 92

Bitcoin Mining Software 96

Bitcoin Cloud Mining 97

What is Bitcoin Mining? 98

What is Proof of Work? 100

What is Bitcoin Mining Difficulty? 100

The Computationally-Difficult Problem 102

The Bitcoin Network Difficulty Metric 102

The Block Reward 103

Chapter 9: 105

Best Bitcoin Business Ideas & Opportunities 105

Becoming a Bitcoin Broker 106

BTMs: Operating a Bitcoin ATM 107

Bitcoin Vending Machine Businesses 110

White Label Business Opportunities 112

Bitcoin Franchise Opportunities 115

Retail Businesses 117

Reseller & Dropship Opportunities 118

Monetizing Trust: Escrow Agents & Oracles 119

7

Consultancy Businesses 120

Flipping Websites, Apps & Businesses 122

Bitcoin Websites & Faucets 123

Chapter 10: 124

Bitcoin for investment 124

Managing Enormous Risk: Bitcoin and Altcoin Investment Strategies 126

Diversify and play it safe 128

Bet on the idea, not the project 129

Hedging 129

Liquidity, liquidity, liquidity 131

Room to grow 132

Technical analysis 133

Proof of Stake interest 134

The security of Bitcoin 136

Classifications of Bitcoin transactions 136

Find the Bitcoin solution for you 138

If you make many transactions of low value .. 138

If you make many transactions of high value 139

If you make few transactions of high value ... 140

If you make few transactions of low value 142

Chapter 11: 144

Awesome facts about Bitcoin.. 144

Bitcoin Studies 144

Bitcoin Boulevard 145

The first transaction... 145

The million dollar Bitcoin pizza...................... 147

A Bitcoin master swindle 148

More Bitcoin users in Poland than in France 150

64% is the estimated part of present « ghost » Bitcoins on the Blockchain.............................. 151

The computing power of the Bitcoin network is 7468 times higher than the one of the cumulative 500 world supercomputers 152

The largest transaction ever made on the network: 194 993 BTC 154

Bitcoin's Tiger Woods.. 155

Chapter 12: 157

Cryptocurrency market moving beyond bitcoin?.............. 157

What is Ethereum?... 157

Why a decentralized system?............................... 158

Ethereum virtual machine and DApps........... 160

The DAO Hack.. 161

Ethereum Classic... 163

Where can I use ETH?... 164

How do I invest in Ethereum?........................... 165

How to transfer money with Ethereum 166

Making money with Ethereum 167

What to watch out for.. 168

What's next for Ethereum?................................. 169

Ripple.. 171

What is Ripple?.. 171

How is Ripple different from bitcoin?............ 172

Where can I use Ripple?....................................... 174

How do I invest in Ripple?.................................. 175

Using Ripple to transfer money 177

Making money with Ripple................................ 177

Get paid in Ripple.. 178

Invest in Ripple 178

What to watch out for 179

What's next for Ripple? 180

Litecoin 181

What is Litecoin? 182

How is Litecoin different from bitcoin? 182

Where can I use Litecoin? 184

How do I invest in Litecoin? 184

Using Litecoin to transfer money 186

Making money with Litecoin 186

What to watch out for 188

The future of Litecoin 189

Chapter 13: **190**

The Secrets Of Cryptocurrency *190*

CHAPTER 1:

HISTORY OF BLOCKCHAIN

Many of the technologies we now take for granted were quiet revolutions in their time. Just think about how much smartphones have changed the way we live and work. It used to be that when people were out of the office, they were gone because a telephone was tied to a place, not to a person. Now we have global nomads building new businesses straight from their phones. And to think: Smartphones have been around for merely a decade.

We're now in the midst of another quiet revolution: blockchain, a distributed database that maintains a continuously growing list of ordered records, called "blocks." Consider what's happened in just the past 10 years:

• The first major blockchain innovation was bitcoin, a digital currency experiment. The market cap of bitcoin now hovers between $10–$20 billion dollars and is used by millions of people for payments, including a large and growing remittances market.

The second innovation was called blockchain, which was essentially the realization that the underlying technology that operated bitcoin could be separated from the currency and used for all kinds of other inter-organizational cooperation. Almost every major financial institution in the world is doing blockchain research at the moment, and 15% of banks are expected to be using blockchain in 2017.

The third innovation was called the "smart contract," embodied in a second-generation blockchain system called ethereum, which built little computer programs directly into blockchain that allowed financial instruments, like loans or bonds, to be represented, rather than only the cash-like tokens of the bitcoin. The ethereum smart contract platform now has a market cap of around a billion dollars, with hundreds of projects headed toward the market.

The fourth major innovation, the current cutting edge of blockchain thinking, is called "proof of stake." Current generation blockchains are secured by "proof of work," in which the group with the largest total computing power makes the decisions. These groups are called "miners" and operate vast data centers to provide this security, in exchange for cryptocurrency payments. The new systems do away with these data centers, replacing them with complex financial instruments, for a similar or even higher degree of security. Proof-of-stake systems are expected to go live later this year.

The fifth major innovation on the horizon is called blockchain scaling. Right now, in the blockchain world, every computer in the network processes every transaction. This is slow. A scaled blockchain accelerates the process, without sacrificing security, by figuring out how many computers are necessary to validate each transaction and dividing up the work efficiently. To manage this without compromising the legendary security and robustness of blockchain is a difficult problem, but not an intractable one. A scaled blockchain is expected to be fast enough to power the internet of things and go head-to-head with the major payment middlemen (VISA and SWIFT) of the banking world.

This innovation landscape represents just 10 years of work by an elite group of computer scientists, cryptographers, and mathematicians. As the full potential of these breakthroughs hits society, things are sure to get a little weird. Self-driving cars and drones will use blockchains to pay for services like charging stations and landing pads. International currency transfers will go from taking days to an hour, and then to a few minutes, with a higher degree of reliability than the current system has been able to manage.

These changes and others represent a pervasive lowering of transaction costs. When transaction costs drop past invisible thresholds, there will be sudden, dramatic, hard-to-predict aggregations and disaggregations of existing business models. For example, auctions used to be narrow and local, rather than universal and global, as they are now on sites like eBay. As the costs of reaching people dropped, there was a sudden change in the system. The blockchain is reasonably expected to trigger as many of these cascades as e-commerce has done since it was invented, in the late 1990s.

Predicting what direction it will all take is hard. Did anybody see social media coming? Who would have predicted that clicking on our friends' faces would replace time spent in front of the TV? Predictors usually overestimate how fast things will happen and underestimate the long-term impacts. But the sense of scale inside the blockchain industry is that the changes coming will be "as large as the original invention of the internet," and this may not be overstated. What we can predict is that as blockchain matures and more people catch on to this new mode of collaboration, it will extend into everything from supply chains to provably fair internet dating (eliminating the possibility of fake profiles and other underhanded techniques). And given how far blockchain come in 10 years, perhaps the future could indeed arrive sooner than any of us think.

Until the late 1990s, it was impossible to process a credit card securely on the internet — e-commerce simply did not exist. How fast could blockchain bring about another revolutionary change? Consider that Dubai's blockchain strategy is to issue all government documents on blockchain by 2020, with substantial initial projects just announced to go live this year. The

Internet of Agreements concept presented at the World Government Summit builds on this strategy to envision a substantial transformation of global trade, using blockchains to smooth out some of the bumps caused by Brexit and the recent U.S. withdrawal from the Trans-Pacific Partnership. These ambitious agendas will have to be proven in practice, but the expectation in Dubai is that cost savings and innovation benefits will more than justify the cost of experimentation. As Mariana Mazzucato teaches in The Entrepreneurial State, the cutting edge of innovation, particularly in infrastructure, is often in the hands of the state, and that seems destined to be true in the blockchain space.

CHAPTER 2:

INTRODUCTION TO BLOCKCHAIN

Crypto-what? If you've attempted to dive into this mysterious thing called blockchain, you'd be forgiven for recoiling in horror at the sheer opaqueness of the technical jargon that is often used to frame it. So before we get into what a cryptocurrency is and how blockchain technology might change the world, let's discuss what blockchain actually is.

In the simplest terms, a blockchain is a digital ledger of transactions, not unlike the ledgers we have been using for hundreds of years to record sales and purchases. The function of this digital ledger is, in fact, pretty much identical to a traditional ledger in that it records debits and credits between people. That is the core concept behind blockchain; the difference is who holds the ledger and who verifies the transactions.

With traditional transactions, a payment from one person to another involves some kind of intermediary to facilitate the transaction. Let's say Rob wants to transfer £20 to Melanie. He can either give her cash in the form of a £20 note, or he can use some kind of banking app to transfer the money directly to her bank account. In both cases, a bank is an intermediary verifying the transaction: Rob's funds are verified when he takes the money out of a cash machine, or they are verified by the app when he makes the digital transfer. The bank decides if the transaction should go ahead. The bank also holds the record of all transactions made by Rob and is solely responsible for updating it whenever Rob pays someone or receives money into his account. In other words, the bank holds and controls the ledger, and everything flows through the bank.

That's a lot of responsibility, so it's important that Rob feels he can trust his bank otherwise he would not risk his money with them. He needs to feel confident that the bank will not defraud him, will not lose his money, will not be robbed, and will not disappear overnight. This need for trust has underpinned pretty much every major behaviour and facet of the monolithic finance industry, to the extent that even when it was discovered that banks were being irresponsible with our money during the financial crisis of 2008, the government (another intermediary) chose to bail them out rather than risk destroying the final fragments of trust by letting them collapse.

Blockchains operate differently in one key respect: they are entirely decentralized. There is no central clearing house like a bank, and there is no central ledger held by one entity. Instead, the ledger is distributed across a vast network of computers, called nodes, each of which holds a copy of the entire ledger on their respective hard drives. These nodes are connected to one another via a piece of software called a peer-to-peer (P2P) client, which synchronizes data across the network of nodes and makes sure that everybody has the same version of the ledger at any given point in time.

When a new transaction is entered into a blockchain, it is first encrypted using state-of-the-art cryptographic technology. Once encrypted, the transaction is converted to something called a block, which is basically the term used for an encrypted group of new transactions. That block is then sent (or broadcast) into the network of computer nodes, where it is verified by the nodes and, once verified, passed on through the network so that the block can be added to the end of the ledger on everybody's computer, under the list of all previous blocks. This is called the chain, hence the tech is referred to as a blockchain.

Once approved and recorded into the ledger, the transaction can be completed. This is how cryptocurrencies like Bitcoin work.

Accountability and the removal of trust

What are the advantages of this system over a banking or central clearing system? Why would Rob use Bitcoin instead of normal currency?

The answer is trust. As mentioned before, with the banking system it is critical that Rob trusts his bank to protect his money and handle it properly. To ensure this happens, enormous regulatory systems exist to verify the actions of the banks and ensure they are fit for purpose. Governments then regulate the regulators, creating a sort of tiered system of checks whose sole purpose is to help prevent mistakes and bad behavior. In other words, organizations like the Financial Services Authority exist precisely because banks can't be trusted on their own. And banks frequently make mistakes and misbehave, as we have seen too many times. When you have a single source of authority, power tends to get abused or misused. The trust relationship between people and banks is awkward and precarious: we don't really trust them but we don't feel there is much alternative.

Blockchain systems, on the other hand, don't need you to trust them at all. All transactions (or blocks) in a blockchain are verified by the nodes in the network before being added to the ledger, which means there is no single point of failure and no single approval channel. If a hacker wanted to successfully tamper with the ledger on a blockchain, they would have to simultaneously hack millions of computers, which is almost impossible. A hacker would also be pretty much unable to bring a blockchain network down, as, again, they would need to be able to shut down every single computer in a network of computers distributed around the world.

The encryption process itself is also a key factor. Blockchains like the Bitcoin one use deliberately difficult processes for their verification procedure. In the case of Bitcoin, blocks are verified by nodes performing a deliberate processor- and time-intensive series of calculations, often in the form of puzzles or complex mathematical problems, which mean that verification is neither instant nor accessible. Nodes that do commit the resource to verification of blocks are rewarded with a transaction fee and a bounty of newly-minted Bitcoins. This has the function of both incentivizing people to become nodes (because processing blocks like this require pretty powerful computers and a lot of electricity), whilst also handling the process of generating - or minting - units of the currency. This is referred to as mining because it involves a considerable amount of effort (by a computer, in this case) to produce a new commodity. It also means that transactions are verified by the most independent way possible, more independent than a government-regulated organization like the FSA.

This decentralized, democratic and highly secure nature of blockchains means that they can function without the need for regulation (they are self-regulating), government or other opaque intermediary. They work because people don't trust each other, rather than in spite of.

Let the significance of that sink in for a while and the excitement around blockchain starts to make sense.

Smart contracts

Where things get really interesting is the applications of blockchain beyond cryptocurrencies like Bitcoin. Given that one of the underlying principles of the blockchain system is the secure, independent verification of a transaction, it's easy to imagine other ways in which this type of process can be valuable. Unsurprisingly, many such applications are already in use or development. Some of the best ones are:

• **Smart contracts (Ethereum):** probably the most exciting blockchain development after Bitcoin, smart contracts are blocks that contain code that must be executed in order for the contract to be fulfilled. The code can be anything, as long as a computer can execute it, but in simple terms, it means that you can use blockchain technology (with its independent verification, trustless architecture and security) to create a kind of escrow system for any kind of transaction. As an example, if you're a web designer you could create a contract that verifies if a new client's website is launched or not, and then automatically release the funds to you once it is. No more chasing or invoicing. Smart contracts are also being used to prove ownership of an asset such as property or art. The potential for reducing fraud with this approach is enormous.

- **Cloud storage (Storj)**: cloud computing has revolutionized the web and brought about the advent of Big Data which has, in turn, kick-started the new AI revolution. But most cloud-based systems are run on servers stored in single-location server farms, owned by a single entity (Amazon, Rackspace, Google etc). This presents all the same problems as the banking system, in that your data is controlled by a single, opaque organization which represents a single point of failure. Distributing data on a blockchain removes the trust issue entirely and also promises to increase reliability as it is so much harder to take a blockchain network down.

- **Digital identification (ShoCard):** two of the biggest issues of our time are identified theft and data protection. With vast centralized services such as Facebook holding so much data about us, and efforts by various developed-world governments to store digital information about their citizens in a central database, the potential for abuse of our personal data is terrifying. Blockchain technology offers a potential solution to this by wrapping your key data up into an encrypted block that can be verified by the blockchain network whenever you need to prove your identity. The applications of this range from the obvious replacement of passports and I.D. cards to other areas such as replacing passwords. It could be huge.

- **Digital voting**: highly topical in the wake of the investigation into Russia's influence on the recent U.S. election, digital voting has long been suspected of being both unreliable and highly vulnerable to tampering. Blockchain technology offers a way of verifying that a voter's vote was successfully sent while retaining their anonymity. It promises not only to reduce fraud in elections but also to increase general voter turnout as people will be able to vote on their mobile phones.

Blockchain technology is still very much in its infancy and most of the applications are a long way from general use. Even Bitcoin, the most established blockchain platform, is subject to huge volatility indicative of its relative newcomer status. However, the potential for blockchain to solve some of the major problems we face today makes it an extraordinarily exciting and seductive technology to follow. I will certainly be keeping an eye out.

Chapter 3:

How Blockchain Technology Can Benefit Many Industries Beyond Finance

Blockchain technology is largely associated with the financial sector, but distributed ledger applications have much to offer other industries as well.

Deloitte University Press recently released a report titled, "Beyond bitcoin, blockchain is coming to disrupt your industry," examining blockchain's application in different industries. Industries besides the financial sector include media, consumer products, industrial products, automobiles, travel, hospitality, retail, life sciences, healthcare, government, and energy.

The report, authored by David Schatsky and Craig Muraskin, reviews the history and workings of blockchain technology. It noted that $1 billion venture capital has been invested in more than 120 block-chain related startups, half of which has occurred in a recent 12-month period.

FINANCIAL SECTOR LEADS

24/7 Instant Spot Trading.

The current method for spot trading is not instantaneous. Even though the idea behind spot trading is for immediate delivery of the traded instrument, it actually takes a day or two to settle the majority of transactions. This is because of the delay associated with using third parties in each transaction, such as brokers. As a result of the involvement of these intermediaries, one cannot currently spot trade on the weekends.

The blockchain database can get around this problem, by introducing direct trading between clients that doesn't necessitate using third parties to settle the transaction. This means that trade contracts can be settled immediately, reducing settlement costs and providing a highly liquid market at all times, including on the weekends.

Another crucial point is that instantaneous trading will almost eliminate counter-party risk. This is the risk that one party in a trade defaults while the transaction is in the process of settlement. It's little wonder that financial institutions are excited about this benefit of blockchain technology.

Cheaper Banking.

Banks are also optimistic about the cost reduction benefits of blockchain technology. A key area of banking that the distributed database will save money on is international payments. In traditional banking, international payments can take up to four days to settle. The current architecture results in the need for centralized authorities to verify transactions. This verification takes time, and it is expensive for banks.

With blockchain technology, both parties can reach an agreement on the validity of a transaction, without the need for a bureaucratic authority. This agreement would be instantaneous because each bank will have its own copy of the blockchain ledger. The payment could be verified by every computer on the network in less than a few minutes, and thus recognized as a valid transaction.

Instantaneous international payments would reduce costs for banks enormously, and give them a serious boost in terms of efficiency. It's no surprise that some major banks are already looking at ways to implement the blockchain within a few years.

Media And Telecom Uses

Beyond the financial sector, the media and telecommunication industries offer use cases. Media sector applications include supporting low-cost micro-transactions that can be processed without the fees that existing payment networks require. A newspaper website, for example, can charge readers per page or per article rather than per month.

The blockchain can secure intellectual property and creative digital products like music and images. A blockchain ledger can be a reliable and secure way to prove a work's provenance and attribution. The digital block's programmability makes it possible to enforce usage rights.

IBM and Samsung have offered a proof-of-concept built partly using Ethereum, a blockchain-base framework, to demonstrate how blockchain can support the Internet of Things (IoT) applications by supporting transaction processing devices. The distributed nature of the ledger can foster coordination among multiple devices.

In addition, the cryptographic security that blockchains rely on can reduce the security challenges that IoT deployments face.

Verizon Ventures, a division of Verizon Communications, has invested in a startup that has raised $5 million is exploring blockchain-enabled IoT applications. Orange, a telecom, has also invested in a blockchain startup.

Alternative retail payment platforms are the most obvious application in the consumer and industrial products arenas.

Other applications are more futuristic. DocuSign, which provides digital transaction management and electronic signature technology, developed an app for Visa's "connected car" proof of concept. The app integrates with the bitcoin blockchain and records contracts. The application is designed to simplify auto purchasing and leasing.

TRAVEL AND HOSPITALITY USES

For travel and hospitality, a shared distributed ledger can simplify the settlement process. Blockchain technology can support loyalty points programs that include a more advantageous accounting of liabilities created by the accrual of points, real-time updating of points balances, and improved points management across franchised operations.

In healthcare and life sciences, blockchain technology can secure digital assets. Factom, a blockchain-based record-keeping service, has partnered with medical procedure billing and ordering services. The partnerships will use blockchain to store healthcare records. The cryptographic security can enhance records security while the irrevocable and immutable nature of transactions can make claims processing more efficient.

Blockchain-secured health records could make it easier for patients to share records with numerous providers while keeping control of the records. Philips Healthcare is exploring applications for blockchain technology, but it has not disclosed the applications it is evaluating.

Public Sector Uses

The blockchain can improve record keeping in the public sector. Factom has reportedly partnered with the Honduras government on a blockchain program to record land ownership. The program's goal is to reduce fraud and corruption associated with a government-controlled centralized registry by substituting that system with a transparent, distributed ledger.

Other public sector uses include vehicle registries, digital identities for individuals, voting records and benefits disbursements.

In the energy sector, a South African company integrated bitcoin payments into smart utility meter reading to enable customers to prepay utility bills digitally. This system is especially helpful for unbanked customers, and it is easier to administer.

Horizontal blockchain applications apply to numerous industries. Such applications include automated audits, smart contracts and enhanced cybersecurity.

Smart contracts – agreements that can automatically activate actions based on specific conditions – could reduce administrative costs by "self-enforcing," such as requiring a driver to be current on lease payments in order to start a leased car.

Blockchain technology can change the role of corporate audits by allowing a third party to verify a distributed network to ensure the transactions are accurate, complete and unalterable.

Cryptographic signing using blockchain can enable immediate detection of data manipulation and verify IT system integrity, giving blockchain a role in cybersecurity. Guardtime, a company based in Estonia, has explored such a solution.

TOP THREE BLOCKCHAIN ECOSYSTEM SEGMENTS

The report divides the blockchain vendor ecosystem into three categories.

1. Applications and solutions providers include bitcoin wallet operators and payment providers.

2. Middleware and services include software platforms that allow enterprises to build

blockchain applications. Such companies include Factom, BlockCypher, Colu and Chain Inc.

3. Infrastructure and protocols players seek to use blockchain technology to create cryptographically-secure, distributed consensus mechanisms. Examples include Ethereum, an open source, crowdfunded project that has become a bitcoin blockchain alternative. Ripple has also developed its own distributed ledger technology. The infrastructure and protocols segment has secured just under $300 million in venture funding, two-thirds of which occurred in 2015.

Investment is shifting toward the middleware and infrastructure providers versus bitcoin, the report noted.

It may be a year or more before significant commercial applications of the technology emerge, but it is increasingly likely that over time many industries will experience its impact.

CHAPTER 4:

THE FUTURE OF BLOCKCHAIN

Society is transforming at an unprecedented rate: from rewriting the traditional social contract between government and citizens, to online retailers waging war against bricks-and-mortar, these changes are building blocks to a new economic reality.

The sharing economy has the potential to bring about renewed trust in the advantages of globalization and to speed up economic development worldwide. For the time being it's also missing an infrastructure that builds trust and which does not rely on a centralized system. Blockchain, supporting distributed ledger technology (DLT), could grow into that infrastructure, and thus enable fast and trusted exchanges in a decentralized network. Businesses and governments alike are currently investigating the potential of blockchain. It will be critical that they maintain a holistic view of the risks and opportunities that DLT technology holds beyond their specific industry, supply chain or regulatory focus.

MY BLOCKCHAIN, YOUR BLOCKCHAIN

A highly versatile technology, blockchain can be designed to match the exact requirements of its users. At the same time, it is important to understand the trade-offs and limitations of deploying the technology, particularly at scale. Blockchain should not be considered as a single technology solution that can solve all problems.

In a report released earlier this year Data61, the CSIRO's research lab examined the risks and opportunities for three use cases for blockchains, being supply chain, open registry, and payment systems. In the report, Data61 highlighted a number of the currently known limitations to blockchain implementations. For example, it noted that current blockchain systems such as Bitcoin cannot match the maximum throughput of conventional transaction processing systems, which raises the issue of scalability. Similarly, the fact that all data on the blockchain is publicly readable and immutable raises potential issues about confidentiality and the ability to erase information. The report also noted that some of these limitations (such as scalability) are the subject of research and developments which may be addressed in the future, but some of the limitations are an inherent property of blockchains.

INTERACTION WITH THE LAW

Versatility is one of the blockchain's key advantages. The technology can be adapted to most sectors of activity, and to a large share of processes that do not involve sensitive information or require human oversight. Most industries have jumped on the blockchain development bandwagon, and according to independent sources banks are expected to quintuple their investment in the technology over the next two years. The technology is bringing together finance and insurance companies, while other sectors such as healthcare and agriculture are also investigating the technology's capabilities.

At this time, interest in potential blockchain applications includes enabling payments and financial transactions, actioning "smart contracts", and managing complex supply chains. While blockchain can support a decentralized and trusted open database with immutable transactions, there are several legal risk areas which private business should take into account:

PRIVACY AND CONFIDENTIALITY

At its core, blockchain is a distributed database that allows any participating node to retrieve and verify its content. All data in this database is accessible to any participating node. While data stored on the blockchain can be (and generally is) stored encrypted or in a de-identified way (for example, a BitCoin address consists of nothing more than a string of random-looking alphanumeric characters), the transactions on the blockchain are readable (so that participating nodes can process and verify the transactions). For example, a processing node will be able to determine that address A sent 5 BitCoins to address B at a particular time (but will not be able to tell the identity of the person in control of address A and address B). While de-identification is a useful means to protect privacy, the risk of re-identification through data-matching will need to be considered, especially over the long term. For example, if the owner of address A is identified (at any time), then all BitCoin transactions made by that address A will be associated with that person. In BitCoin, this privacy risk can be addressed by the user not reusing any BitCoin addresses. Another way to address the privacy risk is to operate a permissioned blockchain that only permits trusted entities to process (and therefore view) the blockchain.

HUGE POTENTIAL

In business today, we still require trusted administrators to manage and record the numbers and databases – auditors, supervisory boards and so on. The potential of blockchain is that it offers the chance to "distribute" these digital ledgers to others through a network of computers across the world. It could actually dispense with those businesses that are based on trusted relationships – such as banking, auditing, solicitors, even aspects of government. For example in Sweden, Georgia and Ukraine property registers are being moved on to the blockchain.

In finance, people rarely lend directly to each other, hence the need for banks as trusted go-betweens. The beauty of cryptocurrencies such as bitcoin or ethereum is that they remove the need for the trusted third party, using instead an encrypted, secure database. This has huge implications for any business that requires the verification of payments and performance of contracts – that is, most businesses.

The beauty of blockchain is that something can be unique and stored digitally with ease, without needing an equivalent in the real world. For example, things like contracts, wills, deeds and share certificates might only require a piece of code stored on the blockchain that represents the exchange. Instead of a trusted intermediary verifying transactions, the computers of the shared network of bitcoin users themselves perform the verification at no cost to those involved in the transaction.

Lack of Identity and Verification

In conventional transactions, trust between the parties is generally established through identity verification. Similarly, identity verification is a core aspect of the 'know your client' requirement that applies to many businesses and transactions. Blockchain implementations are naturally geared towards enabling automated processing where the identity of the underlying actors are not relevant or automatically masqueraded. While identity can be verified separately and linked to the on-chain data, this creates privacy risks as described above.

Permanency and Irreversibility

By its nature, a blockchain is an ever-growing sequential chain of chronological transactions that are linked to the rules implemented in that blockchain.

For example, reversing an incorrect transaction on a blockchain requires a new transaction (which must generally be initiated by the relevant user, given the decentralized nature of blockchain) to reverse the economic effect of the old transaction, rather than deleting the old transaction. While this permanency is beneficial in many use cases, it may not be appropriate for certain use cases. For example, in the case of a fraudulent transaction involving a blockchain-based asset registry or BitCoin, the court may order the reversal of the transaction, but the lack of central control means that the enforcement of that order is difficult if the fraudulent actor cannot be found or compelled to initiate the reverse transaction. At present, such issue can be addressed by creating a 'fork' of the blockchain, but that requires consensus of the community and may result in a fractured community. Developments are also being made to develop blockchains that can be edited in certain circumstances, but such a model requires a central administrator, which removes the benefits of a fully decentralized model.

Enforceability and Relative Trust

This verification process holds the seeds of change across huge numbers of industries. The distributed ledger – the blockchain – offers the chance to enhance truth and trust in every system to which it is applied. It can prove who owns what at any given moment. Anything that currently exists to verify contracts, ownership, payments and even performance can be shifted to the blockchain.

This would transfer power away from those who currently manage or verify transactions – a seismic change to the way the world currently operates. As with any power shift, those holding power are reluctant to surrender it. The "winners" in this scenario will come from existing companies rather than start-ups, given that for this new system to work, it requires buy-in and trust – existing brands already have this advantage.

So what are blockchain's main advantages? By performing the functions of record keepers and managers it would enhance decentralization, reduce the number of intermediaries involved and provide an alternative to how value can be stored. Physical as well as digital assets could be uniquely verified online to prove ownership.

As transactions stored on the blockchain could be independently verified and traced, it would be easier to fight crime, counterfeiting and fraud, reducing systemic risk in the financial system. A distributed digital ledger would make it near impossible to change or falsify data because data would have to be altered across all the related "blocks" in the digital chain, so any tampering would be exposed. Consequently, associated costs would fall, enhance economic growth and prosperity.

A dramatic disruption is happening already in the financial industry: the world's largest custodian bank, BNY Mellon, is using a blockchain based platform for government bond settlement. And one of the Bank of England's research focus areas is based on financial technology or "fintech" and how it affects the way markets and society function.

Another benefit would be to make micropayments possible digitally. A country such as India, where a huge number of people still do not have access to banking, could experience profound economic change if brought within their reach, helping them save, borrow and plan for their future.

Intellectual Property

While cost-effective in the long-run, blockchain requires high capital investment in the early stages. Organizations engaging in platform design should protect resulting IP sooner rather than later in the process to avoid issues. However, protection of software IP in the context of blockchain has its own challenges, as participants of the blockchain will likely demand a full copy of the source code and its implementation to satisfy itself that the implementation is sound and reflects the intended operational rules. Many blockchain technologies are also either based on open source software or released as open source software, which further limits the ability to claim exclusive IP protection.

INTERNATIONAL REGULATION

While legislatures will unlikely regulate blockchain as a technology itself, the implementation of blockchain in particular use cases may be the subject of additional regulatory scrutiny (for example, within the financial or health sectors). At this time, we are not aware of any regulations that govern particular blockchain implementation (including BitCoin, which has received a fair degree of regulatory scrutiny in the context of how it sits within existing regulatory frameworks). However, we estimate that with rapid technological development there will come a regulatory change that companies should prepare for.

ON THE PUBLIC RECORD

Public institutions are equally involved in the race to develop blockchain applications. In some cases, national government branches are trialing the use of blockchain to simplify record-keeping and enhance efficiency, such as the projects developed by Sweden, Brazil and Georgia for centralized land registries.

In Australia, while the federal government commissioned the CSIRO's research arm, Data61, to conduct a study into the opportunities and risks presented by blockchain technology, the Victorian government is taking things a step further, by investigating the potential of the technology through its participation in the Australian Digital Currency and Commerce Association.

Taking into account the joint focus of public institutions and private business on developing blockchain solutions in the near future, the idea of public-private partnerships has great potential. Many issues could benefit from such partnerships, amongst them food safety, welfare benefit management and healthcare. An excellent example of a joint initiative involving blockchain is the ID2020 project driven by the UN in partnership with Accenture and Microsoft. The platform in question would be designed to support to creation and documentation of legal identification to over one billion people living without official documents worldwide, which is critical to them accessing a broad range of basic services including education and healthcare.

Dialogue between stakeholders in the public arena and private business can only accelerate innovation and safeguard from potential risks including noncompliance with evolving regulation, and unilateral development of systems rather than co-design of shared platforms.

THROUGH A GLOBAL LENS

The sharing economy has proven its ability to connect French bakers to American foodies, and Australian globetrotters to Peruvian homeowners. If developed with global standards in mind, blockchain has the potential to deliver faster and improved services to citizens and consumers across the globe.

To prove this claim, China is currently conducting a multipronged effort. A variety of state-owned enterprises (including the People's Bank of China and the ICBC) and privately-owned companies including online retailer Alibaba and tourism giant Wanda are racing to develop blockchain applications within their respective industries.

While the results of the blockchain race are yet uncertain, the technology has a clear potential to redesign the way interaction between states, businesses and individuals occur across the globe. Smart risk management, and a holistic view of operational exposures, legal and regulatory issues, and strategic risks, will be key to blockchain delivering measurable value in the future.

Chapter 5:

Blockchain And Finance Industry

The basic rules of the game for creating and capturing economic value were once fixed in place. For years, or even decades, companies pursued the same old business models (usually selling goods or services, building and renting assets and land, and offering people's time as services) and tried to execute better than their competitors did. But now, business model disruption is changing the very nature of economic returns and industry definitions. All industries are seeing rapid displacement, disruption, and, in extreme cases, outright destruction. The financial services industry, with its large commercial and investment banks and money managers, is no exception.

"Silicon Valley is coming," JPMorgan Chase CEO Jamie Dimon warned in his annual letter to shareholders. He said startups are coming for Wall Street, innovating and creating efficiency in areas that are important to companies such as JPMorgan, particularly in the lending and payments space.

The payments startup Stripe has a multibillion-dollar valuation and a partnership with Apple Pay. Bitcoin companies and exchanges such as 21 and Coinbase are attracting tens of millions of dollars from venture capitalists. Peer-to-peer lending is booming in the small loan market with many players, including Upstart, Prosper, Funding Circle, and more. And the financial-planning startup LearnVest just got acquired for more than $250 million.

Many of these organizations are in the lending business, but are using big data and cloud technologies rather than tellers and branches to speed lending and customer acquisition. Others are leveraging network business models, such as peer-to-peer lending, to bring together would-be lenders and borrowers. According to Dimon, "We are going to work hard to make our services as seamless and competitive as theirs." His underlying thought is this: If his company doesn't keep pace with today's well-capitalized upstarts, they will begin to lose relevance in a platform-centric world.

"In lots of areas, it looks like the blockchain will replace the current centralized business model of the financial services industry."

There are many innovative, network business models that are coming after traditional financial services and banking organizations, and big banks are beginning to realize they must evolve in response if they want to remain viable in a digitally centric world — whether it comes by acquiring, partnering or developing leading-edge technologies. But what's less clear is why, exactly, these new entrants are so disruptive and powerful. What enables them to skirt perceived constraints of these once 'too large to fail' incumbents and exploit unseen possibilities? In short, it is network-centered thinking with platform-based business models.

CONTROL SHIFTING AWAY FROM CENTRAL BANKS

In London's Canary Wharf, a team of technologists and executives are trying to understand how to use blockchain technology to change the future of banking globally. Their leader is Blythe Masters, an ex-Wall Street commodities trader turned digital entrepreneur focused on turning the mental model and business model of the massive financial services industry and all its related parties (consumers, lawyers, accountants) on its head.

Bank executives worldwide are trying to figure out what this evolution in technology will mean for their firms. "We could go the way that file transfer technology changed music, allowing new businesses like iTunes to emerge. That is why there is such feverish activity at the moment," said Michael Harte, chief operations and technology officer at Barclays, according to a recent article in The Financial Times.

For the massive financial services sector, blockchain technology (the software behind the digital currency, Bitcoin) offers an opportunity to overhaul its existing business model, including its banking infrastructure, approach to settlements and customer interactions. But acting on this opportunity, and making the most of the blockchain, is no easy task given the core beliefs and reinforcing systems that are embedded in the industry.

NETWORKS ARE TAKING OVER

What is the blockchain? It is a distributed database of computers that maintain records and manages transactions. Rather than having a central authority (such as a bank), blockchain uses the network to approve "blocks," or transactions, which are then added to the "chain" of computer code. Cryptography is used to keep transactions secure, and the distributed nature of transaction approval makes the system harder to tamper with.

"It is only a matter of time before the broader financial services and banking industries shift to blockchain and network-based approaches."

Blockchain technology has been hailed by its VC supporters as having revolutionary promise for all involved. "You should be taking this technology as seriously as you should have been taking the development of the Internet in the early 1990's. It's analogous to email for money," said Masters, according to The Financial Times.

And blockchain enthusiasts believe that the application possibilities are endless — improving the way we hold and transfer secure goods from money to deeds to music to intellectual property. In fact, blockchain, as a pure platform technology, may be able to cut out the middlemen (or middle companies) everywhere, even disrupting other disruptors like Airbnb or Uber.

In the present financial services business model, a central ledger most often acts as the custodian of that information (such as the Federal Reserve and its member banks). But in a blockchain world, the information regarding each transaction is transparently held in a digitally shared database in the cloud, without a single central body acting as the middleman. This lack of central authority is the very feature that is turning the current mental and business models of traditional financial institutions on their heads.

In a lot of areas, it looks like the blockchain will replace the current centralized business model of the financial services industry and it is easy to see how it could revolutionize all of Wall Street. The ability of the technology to provide an unforgeable record of identity, including the history of an individual's transactions, is one area being eagerly explored. David Grace, head of global finance at PwC, said that "if you have a secure distributed ledger, it could be used to store validated 'know your customer' data on individuals or companies. ... It's a potentially global application that could provide more security over identity data and where that data are stored."

"It seems that the code can perform better than a real middleman in most cases."

Clearly, we are entering a period of rapid evolution, as the financial services industry determines blockchain and what it means for their business models. Or, another scenario: A slew of startups identifies the possibilities and pulls the rug out from under big institutions. Traditional perceptions about the roles of financial players are already under attack — as it seems that the code can perform better than a real middleman in most cases. Old business models will soon fall prey to the quickly evolving technology and mental models. The network is about to do its magic: Grow and evolve without central control.

NETWORK BUSINESS MODELS WILL DOMINATE

The blockchain is already seeing use outside of the financial services sector, where it got its start. Technology and services giant IBM is adapting the blockchain methodology to develop a currency-less system that could be used for any purpose — for example, executing contracts upon delivery.

Arvind Krishna, senior vice president of IBM Research, believes that in the long run, this technology could facilitate transactions between banks or international businesses. "I want to extend banking to the 3.2 billion people who are going to come into the middle class over the next 15 years," he said. "So I need a much lower cost of keeping a ledger. Blockchain offers some intriguing possibilities there." A firm-centered or centrally controlled banking system clearly will not get him there, and the blockchain will allow him to leverage a digitally-enabled network as the way forward.

Join the Network Revolution

With companies such as IBM and JPMorgan Chase, as well as preeminent venture capitalist firm Andreessen Horowitz, backing this new way of facilitating financial transactions, it is only a matter of time before the broader financial services and banking industries shift to blockchain and network-based approaches Twitter to complement, or replace, the current centralized approach. The question is not whether network business models supported by blockchain technology will disrupt these organizations, but when. So if you are a member of the current financial services industry elite — or a local bank or credit union — it's time to become part of the digital revolution and join the network and platform-emerging world.

CHAPTER 6:

WHAT IS BITCOIN?

Bitcoin is a virtual currency. It doesn't exist in the kind of physical form that the currency & coin we're used to exist in. It doesn't even exist in a form as physical as Monopoly money. It's electrons - not molecules.

But consider how much cash you personally handle. You get a paycheck that you take to the bank - or it's auto-deposited without you even seeing the paper that it's not printed on. You then use a debit card (or a checkbook, if you're old school) to access those funds. At best, you see 10% of it in a cash form in your pocket or in your pocketbook. So, it turns out that 90% of the funds that you manage are virtual - electrons in a spreadsheet or database.

But wait - those are U.S. funds (or those of whatever country you hail from), safe in the bank and guaranteed by the full faith of the FDIC up to about $250K per account, right? Well, not exactly. Your financial institution may only require to keep 10% of its deposits on deposit. In some cases, it's less. It lends the rest of your money out to other people for up to 30 years. It charges them for the loan and charges you for the privilege of letting them lend it out.

How does money get created?

Your bank gets to create money by lending it out.

Say you deposit $1,000 with your bank. They then lend out $900 of it. Suddenly you have $1000 and someone else has $900. Magically, there's $1900 floating around where before there was only a grand.

Now say your bank instead lends 900 of your dollars to another bank. That bank in turn lends $810 to another bank, which then lends $720 to a customer. Poof! $3,430 in an instant - almost $2500 created out of nothing - as long as the bank follows your government's central bank rules.

Creation of Bitcoin is as different from bank funds' creation as cash is from electrons. It is not controlled by a government's central bank, but rather by consensus of its users and nodes. It is not created by a limited-mint in a building, but rather by distributed open source software and computing. And it requires a form of actual work for creation. More on that shortly.

Who invented BitCoin?

The first BitCoins were in a block of 50 (the "Genesis Block") created by Satoshi Nakamoto in January 2009. It didn't really have any value at first. It was just a cryptographer's plaything based on a paper published two months earlier by Nakomoto. Nakamoto is an apparently fictional name - no one seems to know who he or she or they is/are.

Who keeps track of it all?

Once the Genesis Block was created, BitCoins have since been generated by doing the work of keeping track of all transactions for all BitCoins as a kind of public ledger. The nodes/computers doing the calculations on the ledger are rewarded for doing so. For each set of successful calculations, the node is rewarded with a certain amount of BitCoin ("BTC"), which are then newly generated into the BitCoin ecosystem. Hence the term, "BitCoin Miner" - because the process creates new BTC. As the supply of BTC increases, and as the number of transactions increases, the work necessary to update the public ledger gets harder and more complex. As a result, the number of new BTC into the system is designed to be about 50 BTC (one block) every 10 minutes, worldwide.

Even though the computing power for mining BitCoin (and for updating the public ledger) is currently increasing exponentially, so is the complexity of the math problem (which, incidentally, also requires a certain amount of guessing), or "proof" needed to mine BitCoin and to settle the transactional books at any given moment. So the system still only generates one 50 BTC block every 10 minutes, or 2106 blocks every 2 weeks.

So, in a sense, everyone keeps track of it - that is, all the nodes in the network keep track of the history of every single BitCoin.

How much is there and where is it?

There is a maximum number of BitCoin that can ever be generated, and that number is 21 million. According to the Khan Academy, the number is expected to top out around the year 2140.

As of, this morning there were 12.1 million BTC in circulation

Your own BitCoin are kept in a file (your BitCoin wallet) in your own storage - your computer. The file itself is proof of the number of BTC you have, and it can move with you on a mobile device.

If that file with the cryptographic key in your wallet gets lost, so does your supply of BitCoin funds. And you can't get it back.

How much is it worth?

The value varies based on how much people think it's worth - just like in the exchange of "real money." But because there is no central authority trying to keep the value around a certain level, it can vary more dynamically. The first BTC were basically worth nothing at the time, but those BTC still exist. As of 11 AM on December 11, 2013, the public value was $906.00 US per BitCoin. When I finished writing this sentence, it was $900.00. Around the beginning of 2013, the value was around $20.00 US. On November 27, 2013 it was valued at more than $1,000.00 US per BTC. So it's kind of volatile at the moment, but it's expected to settle down.

The total value of all BitCoin - as of the period at the end of this sentence - is around 11 billion US dollars.

How can I spend it?

There are hundreds of merchants of all sizes that take BitCoin in payment, from cafes to auto dealerships.

There's even a BitCoin ATM in Vancouver, British Columbia for converting your BTC to cash in Vancouver, BC.

And so?

Money has had a long history - millennia in length. Somewhat recent legend tells us that Manhattan Island was bought for wampum - seashells & the like. In the early years of the United States, different banks printed their own currency. On a recent visit to Salt Spring Island in British Columbia, I spent currency that was only good on the lovely island. The common theme amongst these was a trust agreement amongst its users that that particular currency held value. Sometimes that value was tied directly to something solid and physical, like gold. In 1900 the U.S. tied its currency directly to gold (the "Gold Standard") and in 1971, ended that tie.

Now currency is traded like any other commodity, although a particular country's currency value can be propped up or diminished through actions of their central bank. BitCoin is an alternate currency that is also traded and its value, like that of other commodities, is determined through trade, but is not held up or diminished by the action of any bank, but rather directly by the actions of its users. Its supply is limited and known however, and (unlike physical currency) so is the history of every single BitCoin. Its perceived value, like all other currency, is based on its utility and trust.

As a form of currency, BitCoin not exactly a new thing in Creation, but it certainly is a new way for money to be created.

CHAPTER 7:

BITCOIN MASTERY

The best way to learn about bitcoin is to jump in and get a few in your "pocket" to get a feel for how they work.

Despite the hype about how difficult and dangerous it can be, getting bitcoins is a lot easier and safer than you might think. In a lot of ways, it is probably easier than opening an account at a traditional bank. And, given what has been happening in the banking system, it is probably safer too.

There are a few things to learn: getting and using a software wallet, learning how to send and receive money, learning how to buy bitcoin from a person or an exchange.

PREPARATION

Before getting started, you will need to get yourself a wallet. You can do this easily enough by registering with one of the exchanges which will host wallet for you. And, although I think you are going to want to have one or more exchange wallets eventually, you should start with one on your own computer both to get a better feel for bitcoin and because the exchanges are still experimental themselves. When we get to that stage of the discussion, I will be advising that you get in the habit of moving your money and coins off the exchanges or diversifying across exchanges to keep your money safe.

WHAT IS A WALLET?

It is a way to store your bitcoins. Specifically, it is software that has been designed to store bitcoin. It can be run on your desktop computer, laptop, mobile device (except, as yet, Apple) and can also be made to store bitcoins on things like thumb drives. If you are concerned about being hacked, then that is a good option. Even the Winklevoss* twins, who have millions invested in bitcoin, put their investment on hard drives which they then put into a safety deposit box.

*The Winklevoss twins are the ones who originally had the idea for a social networking site that became Facebook. They hired Mark Zuckerberg who took their idea as his own and became immensely rich.

WHAT DO YOU NEED TO KNOW ABOUT HAVING A BITCOIN WALLET ON YOUR COMPUTER?

Below you can download the original bitcoin wallet, or client, in Windows or Mac format. These are not just wallets, but are in fact part of the bitcoin network. They will receive, store, and send your bitcoins. You can create one or more addresses with a click (an address is a number that looks like this: 1LyFcQatbg4BvT9gGTz6VdqqHKpPn5QBuk). You will see a field where you can copy and paste a number like this from a person you want to send money to and off it will go directly into that person's wallet. You can even create a QR code which will let someone take a picture with an app on their phone and send you some bitcoin. It is perfectly safe to give these out - the address and QR code are both for my donations page. Feel free to donate!

NOTE: This type of wallet acts both as a wallet for you and as part of the bitcoin system. The reason bitcoin works is that every transaction is broadcast and recorded as a number across the entire system (meaning that every transaction is confirmed and made irreversible by the network itself). Any computer with the right software can be part of that system, checking and supporting the network. This wallet serves as your personal wallet and also as a support for that system. Therefore, be aware that it will take up 8-9 gigabytes of your computer's memory. After you install the wallet, it will take as much as a day for the wallet to sync with the network. This is normal, does not harm your computer, and makes the system as a whole more secure, so it's a good idea.

Bitcoin Qt

- The original wallet.

- This is a full-featured wallet: create multiple addresses to receive bitcoins, send bitcoins easily, track transactions, and back up your wallet.

- Outside of the time it takes to sync, this is a very easy to use option.

- Search for Bitcoin Qt wallet download to find their site.

Armory

- Runs on top of Bitcoin Qt, so it has all of the same syncing requirements.

- Armory allows you to back up, encrypt, and the ability to store your bitcoins off line.

- Search for Bitcoin Armory Wallet to find their site.

If you don't want to have that much memory used or don't want to wait for your wallet to sync, there are good wallets that do not make you sync the entire history of bitcoin:

Multibit

- A lightweight wallet that syncs quickly. This is very good for new users.

- Search for Bitcoin Multibit Wallet to find their site.

Electum

- In addition to being quick and light, this wallet allows you to recover lost data using a passcode.

- Search for Bitcoin Electum Wallet to find their site.

After you get the wallet set up, take a few minutes clicking around. Things to look for:

- There will be a page that shows you how many bitcoins are currently in your wallet. Keep in mind that bitcoins can be broken up into smaller pieces, so you may see a decimal with a lot of zeros after it. (Interesting note, 0.00000001 is one Satoshi, named after the pseudonymous creator of bitcoin).

- There will be an area showing what your recent transactions are.

- There will be an area where you can create an address and a QR code (like the one I have above). You don't need the QR code if you don't want it, but if you run a business and you want to accept bitcoin, then all you'll need to do to accept payment is to show someone the QR code, let them take a picture of it, and they will be able to send you some money. You will also be able to create as many addresses as you like, so if you want to track where the money is coming from, you could have a separately labeled address from each one of your payees.

- There will be an area with a box for you to paste a code when you want to send money to someone or to yourself on an exchange or different wallet.

There will be other options and features, but to start out with, these are the items that you should know about.

GETTING YOUR FIRST BITCOINS

Now that you have a wallet, you will, of course, want to test them out.

The very first place to go is http://faucet.bitcoin.st/.

This is a website that gives out small amounts of bitcoin for the purpose of getting people used to using them. The original version of this was run by the lead developer of bitcoin, Gavin Andreson. That site has since closed and this site operates by sending out one or two advertisements a month. You agree to receive those messages by requesting the bitcoins. Copy and paste your new bitcoin address and enter a phone number to which you can receive an SMS. They send out an SMS to be sure that people are not continuously coming back for more since it costs nothing to create a bitcoin address. They will also send out once or twice a month advertisement to support their operation. The amount they send it trivial: 0.0015 BTC (or 1.5 mBTC). However, they process almost immediately and you can check to see that your address and wallet are working. It is also quite a feeling to get that portion of a bitcoin. (Non-disclaimer: I have no connection with this site and receive nothing if you use them. I simply think they are a good way to get your feet wet).

Congratulations! You have just entered the Bitcoin economy.

To get your feet a little wetter, you can go panning for gold. There are a number of services and websites out there that will pay you in bitcoin to do things like go to certain websites, fill out online surveys, or watch sponsored videos. These are harmless, and you can earn a few extra bitcoins this way, but it is important to remember that these are businesses that get paid when people click on the links on their sites. They are essentially kicking back a portion of what they get paid to you. There is nothing illegal, or even immoral about this (you might like what you see and make a purchase!), but they are frequently flashy and may not be completely straightforward. All the ones that I have tried (particularly bitvisitor.com) have paid out as advertised. It is interesting to experiment with these, but even with the likely rise in the value of bitcoin, you won't become a millionaire doing this. So, unless you are an advertisement junkie, I would recommend you move on. If you would like to try, simply Google "free bitcoins" or something along those lines and you will find numerous sites.

BUYING BITCOIN HAND-TO-HAND

Finally, this is going to be the real test of bitcoin. Can people easily trade them back and forth? If this can't happen, then there can't really be a bitcoin economy because retailers won't be able to use it. If retailers can't use it, what earthly good is it? Fortunately, this is not really a problem. iPhone is a bit of a hold out, but many smartphones have apps (mobile wallets) that will read QR codes and allow you to send bitcoin to whomever you want. You can also display a QR code of your address, or even carry a card in your wallet with your QR code to let people send bitcoin to you. Depending on what kind of wallet you have, you can then check to see if the bitcoins have been received.

A COUPLE OF THINGS TO NOTE:

- When you set up your wallet, if you click around a bit, you will see an option to pay a fee to speed transactions. This money becomes available to a bitcoin miner as he/she/they process bitcoin information. The miners doing the work of creating blocks of information keeps the system up to date and secure. The fee is an incentive to the miner to be sure to include your information in the next information block and therefore "verify" it. In the short term, miners are making most of their money by mining new coins (check the section on What Are Bitcoins for more information about this). In the long term, as it gets harder to find new coins, and as the economy increases, the fees will be an incentive for miners to keep creating more blocks and keep the economy going. Your wallet should be set to pay 0 fees as a default, but if you want, you can add a fee to prioritize your transactions. You are under no obligation to pay a fee, and many organizations that process many small transactions (like the ones that pan for gold described above) produce enough fees to keep the miners happy.

- In clicking around your wallet, on the transactions page or linked to specific transactions, you will see a note about confirmations. When you make a transaction, that information is sent out into the network and the network will send back a confirmation that there is no double entry for that bitcoin. It is smart to wait until you get several confirmations before walking away from someone who has paid you. It is actually not very easy to scam someone hand-to-hand like this, and it is not very cost-effective for the criminal, but it can be done.

WHERE CAN YOU BUY BITCOIN LIKE THIS?

• You may have a Bitcoin Meetup in your area.

• You can check out localbitcoins.com to find people near you who are interested in buying or selling.

• Some are trying to start up local street exchanges across the world. These are called Buttonwoods after the first street exchange established on Wall Street in 1792 under a buttonwood tree. See if there is one, or start one, in your area.

- See if you have any friends who would like to try bitcoins out. Actually, the more people who start using bitcoin, the larger and more successful it will become. So please tell two friends!

Some people ask if it is possible to buy physical bitcoins. The answer to this is both a yes and a no. Bitcoin, by its very nature, is a digital currency and has no physical form. However, there are a couple of ways that you can practically hold a bitcoin in your hands:

- Cascascius Coins: These are the brainchild of Mike Caldwell. He mints physical coins and then embeds the private keys for the bitcoins inside them. You can get the private key by peeling a hologram from the coin which will then clearly show that the coin has been tampered with. Mike has gone out of his way to ensure that he can be trusted. These are a good investment strategy as in the years to come it may be that these coins are huge collector's items.

- Paper Wallets: A paper wallet just means that rather than keeping the information for your bitcoin stored in a digital wallet, you print the key information off along with a private key and keep it safe in a safe, in a drawer, or in your mattress (if you like). This is highly recommended and cost effective system for keeping your bitcoin safe. Keep in mind, though, that someone could steal them or if your house burns, they will go with the house and there will be no way to get them back. Really, no different than cash. Also, as with Casascius Coins, they will not really be good for spending until you put them back into the computer.

* There is software to make printing your paper wallets easier. bitcoinpaperwallet.com is one of the best and includes a good tutorial about how to use them.

* The bitcoins are not actually in the wallet, they are still on the web. In fact, the outside of the wallet will have a QR code that will allow you ship coins to the wallet anytime you like.

* The sealed part of the wallet will have the private key without which you cannot access the coins. Therefore, only put as many coins on the wallet as you want to be inaccessible. You will not be able to

whip this thing out and take out a few coins to buy a cup of coffee. Rather, think of it as a piggy bank. To get the money, you have to smash it. It is possible to take out smaller amounts, but at this point the security of the wallet is compromised and it would be easier for someone to steal the coins. Better to have them all in or out.

* People who use paper wallets are usually security conscious, and there are a number of ways for the nefarious in the world to hack your computer. Bitcoinpaperwallet.com gives a lot of good advice about how to print your wallets securely.

Some people have also asked about buying bitcoins on eBay. Yes, it is possible, but they will be far overpriced. So, selling on eBay might seem to be a better option given the extreme markup over market value you might see. But, as with anything that is too good to be true, this is too good to be true. As I will explain in the next section, selling bitcoin this way is just way too risky.

How Not to Buy Bitcoin

In the next section, I am going to explain a couple of key points about buying from Bitcoin Exchanges. Before I do, let me give you a warning.

A short history lesson: When people first started setting up an actual business based on bitcoin, they used all of the tools available to any merchant. They sold by credit card and PayPal. The problem with this business model was quickly spotted: Bitcoin transactions are not reversible by anyone except the recipient of the money. Credit cards and PayPal have strong buyer protection policies that make it relatively easy for people to request a chargeback. So, nefarious individuals realized this and began making purchases of bitcoin and then sooner or later requesting a chargeback. And, since bitcoin is a non-physical product, sent by new and poorly understood technological means, the sellers were not able to contest this. Because of this, sellers stopped accepting credit cards and PayPal.

This was a big problem for the currency: How to move money between buyers and seller? Some business emerged that would credit you with bitcoin if you wired them money. Very often these businesses would give addresses in Albania, Poland, or Russia. The fact is that many of these did work and there are a lot of stories on the forums of people who bought bitcoins this way. But it took a lot of time and in the meantime, the buyer just had to bite his or her fingernails wondering if they would get their bitcoins or kiss their investment goodbye.

I expect that as bitcoin becomes more acceptable and valuable, we are going to see a version of the Nigerian Prince scam. So the warning is this: we now have exchanges and other businesses that allow for moving money easily onto and off of exchanges. Never wire money for bitcoin. It was a short-lived, and well-forgotten, moment in the history of bitcoin.

CHAPTER 8:

BITCOIN MINING

Before we begin...

Before you read further, please understand that most bitcoin users don't mine! But if you do then this Bitcoin miner is probably the best deal. Bitcoin mining for profit is very competitive and volatility in the Bitcoin price makes it difficult to realize monetary gains without also speculating on the price. Mining makes sense if you plan to do it for fun, to learn or to support the security of Bitcoin and do not care if you make a profit. If you have access to large amounts of cheap electricity and the ability to manage a large installation and business, you can mine for a profit.

If you want to get bitcoins based on a fixed amount of mining power, but you don't want to run the actual hardware yourself, you can purchase a mining contract.

Another tool many people like to buy is a Bitcoin debit card which enables people to load a debit card with funds via bitcoins.

WHAT IS BITCOIN MINING?

Bitcoin mining is a lot like a giant lottery where you compete with your mining hardware with everyone on the network to earn bitcoins. Faster Bitcoin mining hardware is able to attempt more tries per second to win this lottery while the Bitcoin network itself adjusts roughly every two weeks to keep the rate of finding a winning block hash to every ten minutes. In the big picture, Bitcoin mining secures transactions that are recorded in Bitcoin's public ledger, the blockchain. By conducting a random lottery where electricity and specialized equipment are the price of admission, the cost to disrupt the Bitcoin network scales with the amount of hashing power that is being spent by all mining participants.

TECHNICAL BACKGROUND

During mining, your Bitcoin mining hardware runs a cryptographic hashing function (two rounds of SHA256) on what is called a block header. For each new hash that is tried, the mining software will use a different number as the random element of the block header, this number is called the nonce. Depending on the nonce and what else is in the block the hashing function will yield a hash which looks something like this:

93ef6f358fbb998c60802496863052290d4c63735b7fe5bdaac821de96a53a9a

You can look at this hash as a really long number. (It's a hexadecimal number, meaning the letters A-F are the digits 10-15.) To ensure that blocks are found roughly every ten minutes, there is what's called a difficulty target. To create a valid block your miner has to find a hash that is below the difficulty target. So if for example the difficulty target is

1000000000000000000000000000000000000000000000000000000000000000 any number that starts with a zero would be below the target, e.g.:

0787a6fd6e0782f7f8058fbef45f5c17fe89086ad4e78a1520d06505acb4522f

If we lower the target to

0100000000000000000000000000000000000000000000000000000000000000

we now need two zeros in the beginning to be under it:

00db27957bd0ba06a5af9e6c81226d74312a7028cf9a08fa125e49f15cae4979

Because the target is such an unwieldy number with tons of digits, people generally use a simpler number to express the current target. This number is called the mining difficulty. The mining difficulty expresses how much harder the current block is to generate compared to the first block. So a difficulty of 70000 means to generate the current block you have to do 70000 times more work than Satoshi Nakamoto had to do generating the first block. To be fair, back then mining hardware and algorithms were a lot slower and less optimized.

To keep blocks coming roughly every 10 minutes, the difficulty is adjusted using a shared formula every 2016 blocks. The network tries to change it such that 2016 blocks at the current global network processing power take about 14 days. That's why, when the network power rises, the difficulty rises as well.

BITCOIN MINING HARDWARE

CPU

In the beginning, mining with a CPU was the only way to mine bitcoins and was done using the original Satoshi client. In the quest to further secure the network and earn more bitcoins, miners innovated on many fronts and for years now, CPU mining has been relatively futile. You might mine for decades using your laptop without earning a single coin.

GPU

About a year and a half after the network started, it was discovered that high end graphics cards were much more efficient at bitcoin mining and the landscape changed. CPU bitcoin mining gave way to the GPU (Graphical Processing Unit). The massively parallel nature of some GPUs allowed for a 50x to 100x increase in bitcoin mining power while using far less power per unit of work.

While any modern GPU can be used to mine, the AMD line of GPU architecture turned out to be far superior to the nVidia architecture for mining bitcoins and the ATI Radeon HD 5870 turned out to be the most cost effective choice at the time.

FPGA

As with the CPU to GPU transition, the bitcoin mining world progressed up the technology food chain to the Field Programmable Gate Array. With the successful launch of the Butterfly Labs FPGA 'Single', the bitcoin mining hardware landscape gave way to specially manufactured hardware dedicated to mining bitcoins.

While the FPGAs didn't enjoy a 50x - 100x increase in mining speed as was seen with the transition from CPUs to GPUs, they provided a benefit through power efficiency and ease of use. A typical 600 MH/s graphics card consumed upwards of 400w of power, whereas a typical FPGA mining device would provide a hashrate of 826 MH/s at 80w of power.

That 5x improvement allowed the first large bitcoin mining farms to be constructed at an operational profit. The bitcoin mining industry was born.

ASIC

The bitcoin mining world is now solidly in the Application Specific Integrated Circuit (ASIC) era. An ASIC is a chip designed specifically to do one thing and one thing only. Unlike FPGAs, an ASIC cannot be repurposed to perform other tasks.

An ASIC designed to mine bitcoins can only mine bitcoins and will only ever mine bitcoins. The inflexibility of an ASIC is offset by the fact that it offers a 100x increase in hashing power while reducing power consumption compared to all the previous technologies.

Unlike all the previous generations of hardware preceding ASIC, ASIC may be the "end of the line" when it comes to disruptive mining technology. CPUs were replaced by GPUs which were in turn replaced by FPGAs which were replaced by ASICs. There is nothing to replace ASICs now or even in the immediate future.

There will be stepwise refinement of the ASIC products and increases in efficiency, but nothing will offer the 50x to 100x increase in hashing power or 7x reduction in power usage that moves from previous technologies offered. This makes power consumption on an ASIC device the single most important factor of any ASIC product, as the expected useful lifetime of an ASIC mining device is longer than the entire history of bitcoin mining.

It is conceivable that an ASIC device purchased today would still be mining in two years if the device is power efficient enough and the cost of electricity does not exceed it's output. Mining profitability is also dictated by the exchange rate, but under all circumstances the more power efficient the mining device, the more profitable it is. If you want to try your luck at bitcoin mining then this Bitcoin miner is probably the best deal.

BITCOIN MINING SOFTWARE

There are two basic ways to mine: On your own or as part of a Bitcoin mining pool or with Bitcoin cloud mining contracts and be sure to avoid Bitcoin cloud mining scams. Almost all miners choose to mine in a pool because it smooths out the luck inherent in the Bitcoin mining process. Before you join a pool, make sure you have a bitcoin wallet so you have a place to store your bitcoins. Next, you will need to join a mining pool and set your miner(s) to connect to that pool. With pool mining, the profit from each block any pool member generates is divided up among the members of the pool according to the amount of hashes they contributed.

How much bandwidth does Bitcoin mining take? If you are using a bitcoin miner for mining with a pool then the amount should be negligible with about 10MB/day. However, what you do need is exceptional connectivity so that you get any updates on the work as fast as possible.

This gives the pool members a more frequent, steady payout (this is called reducing your variance), but your payout(s) can be decreased by whatever fee the pool might charge. Solo mining will give you large, infrequent payouts and pooled mining will give you small, frequent payouts, but both add up to the same amount if you're using a zero fee pool in the long-term.

BITCOIN CLOUD MINING

By purchasing Bitcoin cloud mining contracts, investors can earn Bitcoins without dealing with the hassles of mining hardware, software, electricity, bandwidth or other offline issues.

Being listed in this section is NOT an endorsement of these services and is to serve merely as a Bitcoin cloud mining comparison. There have been a tremendous amount of Bitcoin cloud mining scams.

Hashflare Review: Hashflare offers SHA-256 mining contracts and more profitable SHA-256 coins can be mined while automatic payouts are still in BTC. Customers must purchase at least 10 GH/s.

Genesis Mining Review: Genesis Mining is the largest Bitcoin and scrypt cloud mining provider. Genesis Mining offers three Bitcoin cloud mining plans that are reasonably priced. Zcash mining contracts are also available.

Hashing 24 Review: Hashing24 has been involved with Bitcoin mining since 2012. They have facilities in Iceland and Georgia. They use modern ASIC chips from BitFury deliver the maximum performance and efficiency possible.

What is Bitcoin Mining?

Bitcoin mining is the process of adding transaction records to Bitcoin's public ledger of past transactions. This ledger of past transactions is called the blockchain as it is a chain of blocks. The blockchain serves to confirm transactions to the rest of the network as having taken place.

Bitcoin nodes use the blockchain to distinguish legitimate Bitcoin transactions from attempts to re-spend coins that have already been spent elsewhere.

Bitcoin mining is intentionally designed to be resource-intensive and difficult so that the number of blocks found each day by miners remains steady. Individual blocks must contain a proof of work to be considered valid. This proof of work is verified by other Bitcoin nodes each time they receive a block. Bitcoin uses the hashcash proof-of-work function.

The primary purpose of mining is to allow Bitcoin nodes to reach a secure, tamper-resistant consensus. Mining is also the mechanism used to introduce Bitcoins into the system: Miners are paid any transaction fees as well as a "subsidy" of newly created coins.

This both serves the purpose of disseminating new coins in a decentralized manner as well as motivating people to provide security for the system.

Bitcoin mining is so called because it resembles the mining of other commodities: it requires exertion and it slowly makes new currency available at a rate that resembles the rate at which commodities like gold are mined from the ground.

WHAT IS PROOF OF WORK?

A proof of work is a piece of data which was difficult (costly, time-consuming) to produce so as to satisfy certain requirements. It must be trivial to check whether data satisfies said requirements.

Producing a proof of work can be a random process with low probability, so that a lot of trial and error is required on average before a valid proof of work is generated. Bitcoin uses the Hashcash proof of work.

WHAT IS BITCOIN MINING DIFFICULTY?

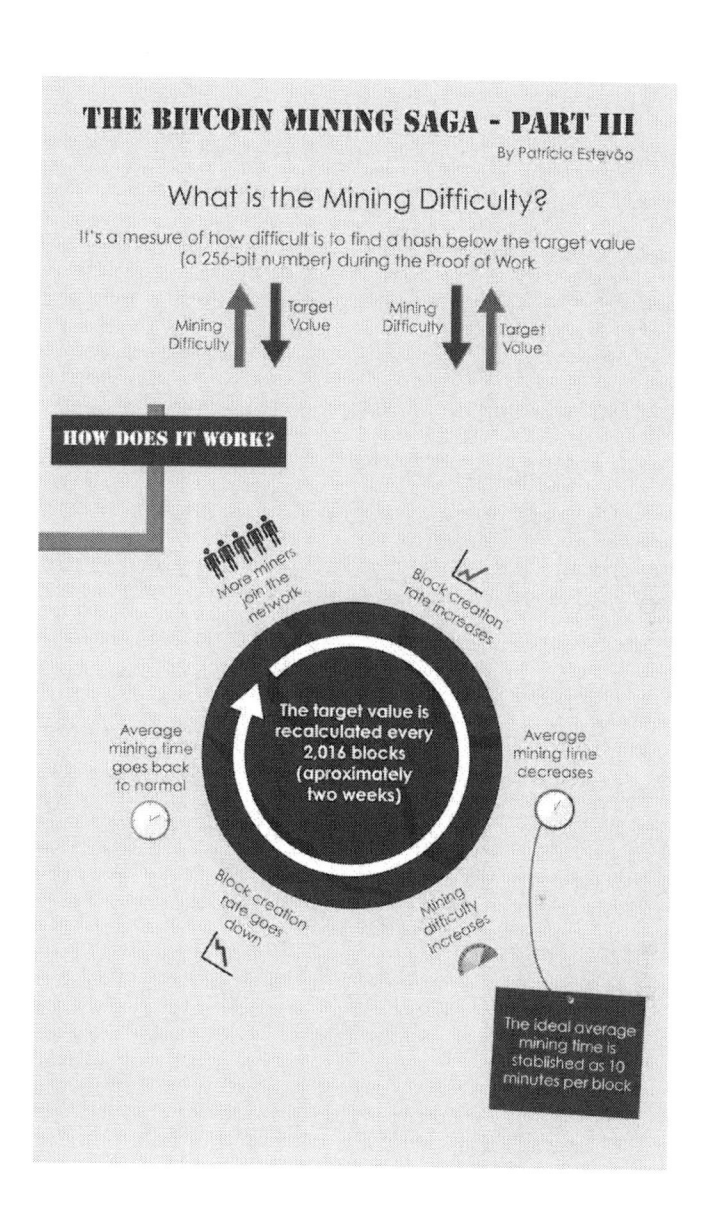

THE BITCOIN MINING SAGA - PART III

By Patrícia Estevão

What is the Mining Difficulty?

It's a mesure of how difficult is to find a hash below the target value (a 256-bit number) during the Proof of Work.

Mining Difficulty ↑ ↓ Target Value

Mining Difficulty ↓ ↑ Target Value

HOW DOES IT WORK?

More miners join the network

Block creation rate increases

Mining difficulty increases

Block creation rate goes down

Average mining time decreases

Average mining time goes back to normal

The target value is recalculated every 2,016 blocks (aproximately two weeks)

The ideal average mining time is stablished as 10 minutes per block

The Computationally-Difficult Problem

Bitcoin mining a block is difficult because the SHA-256 hash of a block's header must be lower than or equal to the target in order for the block to be accepted by the network.

This problem can be simplified for explanation purposes: The hash of a block must start with a certain number of zeros. The probability of calculating a hash that starts with many zeros is very low, therefore many attempts must be made. In order to generate a new hash each round, a nonce is incremented. See Proof of work for more information.

The Bitcoin Network Difficulty Metric

The Bitcoin mining network difficulty is the measure of how difficult it is to find a new block compared to the easiest it can ever be. It is recalculated every 2016 blocks to a value such that the previous 2016 blocks would have been generated in exactly two weeks had everyone been mining at this difficulty. This will yield, on average, one block every ten minutes.

As more miners join, the rate of block creation will go up. As the rate of block generation goes up, the difficulty rises to compensate which will push the rate of block creation back down. Any blocks released by malicious miners that do not meet the required difficulty target will simply be rejected by everyone on the network and thus will be worthless.

THE BLOCK REWARD

When a block is discovered, the discoverer may award themselves a certain number of bitcoins, which is agreed-upon by everyone in the network. Currently, this bounty is 25 bitcoins; this value will halve every 210,000 blocks. See Controlled Currency Supply or use a bitcoin mining calculator.

Additionally, the miner is awarded the fees paid by users sending transactions. The fee is an incentive for the miner to include the transaction in their block. In the future, as the number of new bitcoins miners are allowed to create in each block dwindles, the fees will make up a much more important percentage of mining income.

CHAPTER 9:

BEST BITCOIN BUSINESS IDEAS & OPPORTUNITIES

The use of digital currencies like Bitcoin is continuing to grow around the world, whilst at the same time new applications for the blockchain technology which underpins it are popping up constantly. This creates a huge range of opportunities for entrepreneurs to capitalize on. Establishing your business within a young and growing industry like this may be seen as risky by some, but it also offers the potential for phenomenal growth rates. Personally, I would also suggest that it is an exciting and rewarding business to get into, giving you the chance to be part of something big while helping to take the power bank from the banks and return it to the people.

If you are an entrepreneur (or would like to be one) then I have some good news for you: profitable Bitcoin business ideas are not hard to come by. That doesn't mean that it will be easy for you to make money, or that you are guaranteed success. But that first step of finding interesting opportunities that are worthy of consideration should not be a barrier to anybody willing to invest their time and / or money into digital currency.

In this article you will find a selection of the best 'off-the-shelf' bitcoin business opportunities that you could set up right now, as well as a few more general ideas to help spark the imagination and inspire those among you who prefer to forge your own independent business path

BECOMING A BITCOIN BROKER

Perhaps one of the most obvious as well as one of the most popular ways to start a business in this industry is to set yourself up as a broker, buying and selling coins to other users.

Unlike other areas of finance, digital currency users often have a preference for using peer-to-peer services rather than large companies. This preference extends to exchanges, meaning that it is very easy for a small trader to set themselves up as a broker in their local area or over the internet. In fact, one of the world's most popular services for buying and selling BTC is LocalBitcoins, which is entirely based around peer-to-peer transactions and hosts thousands of small traders earning a living as brokers.

As a broker you earn your profit from the 'spread' – the difference between bid and ask prices. This varies according to market conditions and the payment method you are using, but you can get a rough idea simply by visiting the buy and sell pages on the site for your local area.

BTMs: Operating a Bitcoin ATM

If you have enough capital behind you then a more easily scalable, and potentially more profitable way to set up a business buying and selling coins, is by operating specialist 'Automatic Teller Machines'

(ATMs) sometimes known as 'Bitcoin Teller Machines' (BTM).

Fees charged by BTMs seem to start around the range of 5-10% per transaction, and in some cases are a lot higher. Operators who manage to get their machines into the best locations often report ROI for their initial capital in less than a year. These machines do not take up a lot of space, so renting locations doesn't need to cost the earth. But with the cost of the machine itself, and the requirement to stock it with notes, the initial outlay can be quite high.

There are a wide range of machines available to buy, and they usually allow you to set your own fees to the level you want. Some machines will also allow you to connect to a third-party exchange through an API in order to manage your currency risk by keeping your reserves of both BTC and your local fiat at a constant level. Most machines will incorporate some form of KYC requirements, but it is important for operators to keep abreast of local regulatory requirements and ensure that their machines comply with the law.

If you are already the owner of a retail location then running a BTM may be a particularly attractive proposition, and some systems have been designed with dual-functionality for this reason. Several major BTM manufacturers have included point of sale (POS) systems into their machine, whilst at the same time POS terminal providers such as Coinkite offer exchange features that enable cashiers to buy or sell coins from the till.

Here is a list of some of the most popular options:

- Romit: Kiosks and ATMs with point of sale app and integrated remittance options.

- BitAccess: Fully featuresdATM machines with note recycling, customizable compliance options and remote management.

- GeneralBytes: Offers a choice of full kiosk and combined POS system.

- Skyhook: Powered by open source software, this machine supports a wide range of currencies.

- Lamassu: Offers a range of 3 different machines and is the market leader at the time of writing this article.

- GenesisCoin: Includes the option to brand the product through their white label system, and had all the features you would expect.

There is even a market out there for second hand BTM machines. You can compare products and find cheap second hand deals at CoinATMRadar.

Bitcoin Vending Machine Businesses

There are many similarities between running a network of teller machines and running a vending machine business. Entrepreneurial salespeople with a strong knowledge of their local area can do well by placing these machines in strategic locations.

One of the big limitations of vending machines is that many people simply don't carry a lot of change around with them, and may not have the coins needed to make a purchase. As the use of cash continues to decline this is likely to present an ever-expanding opportunity to replace legacy systems with new machines capable of accepting alternative payment methods.

Already there are machines available to purchase which accept both credit / debit cards and Bitcoin. For example, Aeguana sells a top-spec system with digital display, which they claim has driven an average 400% increase in sales on a like-for-like basis compared to traditional coin operated machines during trials in the UK.

If you don't mind getting your hands dirty (or hiring an engineer) you can also retrofit pretty much any existing vending machine to accept BTC payments using something like the BitSwitch, or alternatively Kryptomechwhich runs its own installation service.

White Label Business Opportunities

A white label business is when another company allows you to take their product or service, rebrand it under your own name, and present it to the public as an independent business. Although the core product is not unique, these services often allow for a relatively high degree of customization.

White Label Exchanges

If you have ever thought of running your own cryptocurrency exchange website, then there are some significant advantages to going through the white label route.

The first is that high quality exchange software capable of reliably matching and executing orders at high speeds is a complex and expensive thing to develop yourself. Setting up a white label exchange is a low cost way to get into this business, but should still allow you to select which coins and currencies you want to trade, set your own fees, and customize the user-interface to suit your brand.

A second major advantage is that these services usually allow you to share liquidity with other exchanges using the same network. Building enough liquidity on a new exchange to make it an attractive choice for users can be very difficult, or very expensive and risky if you provide the liquidity yourself.

Here is a list of the top white label bitcoin exchange providers:

- AlphaPoint

- BTCTrader

- Draglet

- WLox

White Label Casinos

Gambling has always been one of those areas in which the advantages of digital currency are most apparent. One of the reasons for this is because many countries do not classify it as being real money, which means that strict laws and regulations controlling online gambling may not apply to casinos which use BTC exclusively.

If you fancy running your own casino, poker or betting site then there are many white label opportunities for you to take advantage of. These can range from a complete 'turnkey' website which just requires you to add your own branding (and make sure that you are complying with local laws) to individual games that you can add to your own site.

Here are three of the top providers of this service:

1. CoinGaming

2. SoftSwiss
3. BetcoinGaming

Other White Label Services

I'm sure that there are many other white label services out there, offering services other than casinos and exchanges. This is a fast past industry, so it is well worth doing your own search if you think this is something you may like to do. But for now I will leave you with just one other service that you may like to take a look at: E-Coin offers entrepreneurs the chance to white label their bitcoin debit card service, and includes the ability to access their service through an API: https://devportal.e-coin.io/

Bitcoin Franchise Opportunities

Choosing the franchise route means that not only are you provided with a product / service to sell, but you also get access to a proven strategy and business plan, and the rights to use an established brand that may already have name recognition and may run its own advertising campaigns that you can benefit from.

This can be seen as one step up from a white label in terms of the help and support you get from the company behind the product, but you do have to pay for this as there is usually a fee which must be paid to purchase the franchise. If you are considering taking this route then I would advise you to do a little research to find the latest franchise offerings yourself, but to whet your appetite and perhaps save some of you the time and effort, here are three of the most interesting franchises that I have been able to find:

1. Coin Telegraph – One of the most well known names in digital currency news, Coin Telegraph is offering foreign language franchises in many countries around the world. A similar model is being followed by another news site called NewsBTC.
2. Coingaia – A Bitcoin exchange which is using a franchise model instead of the white label

route for anybody looking to start their own exchange.

3. MegaBigPower – If you have been thinking about setting up your own mining business but don't have the full capital outlay required then this is worth looking into. You provide a premises and electricity, and they will provide ASIC mining machines and technical support to help you run them.

Retail Businesses

You can buy most things with Bitcoin today, but there are still opportunities available for new retail businesses which accept digital currency payments to make a name for themselves.

The low transaction costs and freedom from chargebacks makes BTC payments an attractive proposition for retailers, and if you can pass on some of those savings to your customers in the form of discounts you have a great chance to attract new business.

Perhaps the easiest way to set up a new retail business and take payment in BTC is using an internet shop builder service like Shopify.

Reseller & Dropship Opportunities

If you are already involved in retail, or if this is a sector you are thinking about going into, you may also like to consider reselling Bitcoin related products.

For example, Prypto offers a way for retailers to sell Bitcoin in the form of scratch cards or vouchers. This is perfect for adding to the counter of a local newsagent of grocery store, but can also be used by online businesses.

There are also many digital products unrelated to digital currency which have reseller programs. This is a great way to get into retail without a huge expenditure on buying stock, and making a product available to purchase for BTC may win you some business. You can even use a similar method to start selling physical products through 'dropshipping', which involves the retailer taking payment for a product from the customer, and then immediately ordering it from their dropship wholesaler, who ships the product direct to the customer.

Consider selling items on a decentralized marketplace using one of our guides: Syscoin for sellers and Open Bazaar for Merchants.

Monetizing Trust: Escrow Agents & Oracles

If you have built up a name for yourself as somebody that can be trusted (or if your business has), then you may like to consider monetizing this trust by setting yourself up as an escrow agent or oracle.

The role of an escrow agent is the arbitrate over disputes. This may involve online purchases, freelance contracts, or other business and trade arrangements. The process is simple: payment is made to a bitcoin address which requires any 2 signatures out of the buyer, the seller and the escrow agent in order to send a transaction. If there is no problem then the buyer and seller sign and payment is made, but if there is a problem then the escrow agent must choose whether to sign the payment or the refund. You can create a profile on websites like Bitrated to promote your services as an escrow agent.

Another business which requires a certain degree of trust from your customers is the role of the oracle. Oracles publish information over the blockchain which can be used for betting, for financial derivatives, or for smart contracts. Take a look at our article on how to become a bitcoin oracle for more information about this.

Consultancy Businesses

If you are reading this article then you probably know more about bitcoin than 99% of other people, at the very least. So why not put that knowledge to good use by helping other businesses?

Both Bitcoin itself and the blockchain technology which underpins it offer a wealth of opportunities, not only for setting up a new business but also within established businesses. Unfortunately, most companies just don't know how to take advantage of them. This doesn't just stop at accepting Bitcoin payments, it could involve using the blockchain for low cost notary services, as an asset registry, smart contracts and a lot more besides.

Although anybody looking to set themselves up as a consultant must be careful not to overstate their expertise – most general consultancies have teams of people with different backgrounds including programming, law and other areas – there are still profitable niches that anybody with a bit of experience and a willingness to research could take advantage of. For example, approaching small and medium sized retailers in your area and offering to guide them through the various point of sale options, or offering to conduct a presentation on blockchain notary services to a local law firm as a general introduction to what it can offer.

Flipping Websites, Apps &

Businesses

Business flipping is when you buy a business, increase its profitability (or turn it around entirely if its making a loss), and then sell it on in a relatively short period of time. The term is more commonly used for online businesses in the form of website or app flipping, but can also be applied to bricks & mortar businesses.

There are many different websites and apps which could benefit from integrating digital currency into what they offer. It is also possible to buy websites and apps for much less than most other businesses and to 'flip' them within a fairly short period of time. Integrating digital currency for in-app purchases or for user-rewards schemes, or simply converting stores to accept BTC payments, may be worth considering as ways to add value to an established business.

It is not beyond the imagination to think that some offline businesses may present similar opportunities for an entrepreneur to add value in a short space of time by introducing the use of blockchain technology.

BITCOIN WEBSITES & FAUCETS

At the risk of creating more competition for ourselves, another possibility is to create a bitcoin related website. When it comes to monetizing your site, there are many advertising networks and affiliate programs which pay out in bitcoin.

One of the most popular categories of website in this area is the faucet – a website which pays out a small amount of bitcoin to new users for testing or just for fun.

CHAPTER 10:

BITCOIN FOR INVESTMENT

Is Bitcoin a Good Investment?

Questions about the value of bitcoins as an investment will likely differ depending on who you ask. Those with a vision of a fully-distributed future in which the lack of a centralized overseer becomes key to an asset's value will tell you that, yes, bitcoins are poised to become only more valuable in the future. Others who put more value in the traditional trust afforded by banks and government institutions would likely steer you away from bitcoins as an investment.

While determining how "good" any investment will be is ultimately a guessing game, there are some tried and true ways to determine an asset's worth. One of the simplest ways to think about bitcoin as an investment is to consider its rise against the U.S. dollar. Recently, bitcoin prices eclipsed $1,000 and have reached beyond $1,500. If you had invested in the digital currency when its worth was still hovering around $150 just a few years ago, or when it was first introduced in 2009 and worth nothing against the dollar, you would probably be convinced that it made for a good investment.

Furthermore, an underpinning concept behind Bitcoin is that there will only ever be 21,000,000 tokens, meaning that it may stay consistently valuable or increase in value relative to other types of currency which can be printed endlessly. Other reasons that the asset seems like a good investment include its growing popularity, network effects, security, immutability and status as the first ever in a growing world of digital currencies.

That being said, there is at least one significant argument for limiting bitcoins to a small portion of your portfolio at the most. Bitcoin is known for stark jumps in price, high peaks and deep valleys that would make it difficult to have confidence in the asset as a long-term money maker that can be depended on. Tying every dime you have to such a volatile asset would be imprudent. A good rule to follow is never to invest more than what you would be willing to lose.

MANAGING ENORMOUS RISK: BITCOIN AND ALTCOIN INVESTMENT STRATEGIES

While some have made millions investing in digital currencies, others would call it degenerate gambling. If you're reading this, then you know how exciting and unpredictable the crypto world is. Fortunes are built and demolished in seconds, new and exciting technology pops up every day, and controversy rules the land. It's pretty much the Wild West of finance.

The unprecedented growth of cryptocurrencies has attracted investors from all walks of life, many of whom have been enticed by the staggering returns made by early investors. If this sounds like you, then keep reading. Unfortunately, we're not going to teach you how to get rich in a few days; in fact, we're going to try and deter you from that objective.

Not that we don't want you to be super-rich, don't get us wrong. But we prefer to have more grounded goals and we want you to do the same. Investment is a tricky game and the patient person usually wins.

Avoiding "fear of missing out" (FOMO) is essential, especially in crypto, where disinformation, fake news and drama are commonplace.

So what exactly is the point of this article, you may wonder? Well, today, we want to give new players in the cryptosphere some ideas on how they can begin to navigate the tricky world of investment. We feel this is important due to the growing amount of scams and low quality projects out there.

We're not saying that the strategies we discuss are foolproof or even profitable. They are not based on any mathematical formula nor were they devised by an experienced investment professional. These are simple ideas that are popular among entrants and old school digital currency investors alike.

It's important to note that this article is not to be taken as investment advice and that you should always remember the golden rule of investment: Never invest more than what you can afford to lose.

Diversify and Play it Safe

This is a simple one. If your portfolio only has one coin on it, you're doing it wrong. Now, we know some people will say Bitcoin is the only cryptocurrency you should own, but at this point it's safe to say that this is an absurd statement founded on feelings and ideas, rather than actual facts.

Bitcoin is thriving because it is the first and most popular cryptocurrency out there. It has the first mover advantage and it is also backed by an extensive network of miners who keep it safe. In terms of technology or features, however, Bitcoin falls short of its peers. We're not saying you shouldn't have Bitcoin, but you should also acknowledge other cryptocurrencies out there.

It may be a good idea to play it safe, however, and to "bet" on the most popular coins only, such as the top 10 by market capitalization. At present, those are Bitcoin, Ethereum, Ripple, Bitcoin Cash, Litecoin, Dash, NEM, NEO, BitConnect and Monero.

BET ON THE IDEA, NOT THE PROJECT

The world of Blockchain technology has evolved to a point where currency is just one of the many functions a cryptocurrency can have. There are smart contract platforms like Ethereum, NEO and Qtum, there are decentralized storage networks like Storj, Sia Coin and Filecoin and there are decentralized exchange platforms like Waves, Bitshares and others.

Our suggestion is, instead of buying one cryptocurrency in each category, you should spread your investment throughout multiple options inside each category. This will allow you to reduce the risk of investing in one single currency. In the world of crypto, a technical difficulty or even a grievance within one of the teams can lead to a rapid crash in the price, regardless of how promising the project and tech are. Just look at what happened with Tezos.

HEDGING

Again, diversification is the name of the game. If you're in crypto, then you are probably aware of how risky it all is. The cryptocurrency movement could end in days if some major security flaw was discovered or if all governments decided to ban them. The same can happen if some new and improved alternative to Blockchain technology comes along. These are, of course, worse case scenarios that are unlikely but possible nonetheless.

So, if you're not one to have all your eggs in the same basket, you may want to extend your investment strategy to instruments outside of crypto. Precious metals, stocks, and other traditional investment vehicles may be a great addition to your portfolio and will allow you to reduce the risk you would take by investing in cryptocurrencies only.

Some companies, for example, manage cryptocurrency investment funds that combine cryptocurrency investments with investments in other sectors, like real estate. We talked to Kirill Bensonoff, CEO and founder of Caviar, about the importance of heeding your investment in the cryptocurrency space with traditional instruments.

He stated:

"We found a couple of major issues with crypto-asset investing, namely, it's difficult and time consuming, and all assets are highly correlated. There is no 'safety' asset that also produces an income. We also see a movement towards having crypto be backed by traditional assets, such as gold, real estate and others, and we are addressing this head on."

LIqUIDITY, LIQUIDITY, LIqUIDITY

This is something that many new players forget about. You may find yourself investing in a cryptocurrency, having it increase in value several times over, only to realize that you can't really sell it. If you try to sell large amounts at once, you'll crash the price. Why? Because there is no liquidity. If a coin has no trading volume, significant price swings are bound to happen.

You can play it safe and avoid low volume coins all together but if you don't want to, the least you can do is to know the risk you're taking. CryptoCompare has a portfolio tool that allows you to analyze several risk factors in your portfolio, including volatility, exposure and, of course, liquidity. Their tool allows you to get an estimate of how long it would take to sell a certain coin based on the current volume. We asked Charles Hayter, CEO of CryptoCompare, why this tool is important for entrant users. He stated:

"We want to make it easy for users to track how well they're doing. Crypto is risky in the extreme and we want to help people understand where these risks lie and how to quantify them."

ROOM TO GROW

Remember what we just told you about liquidity? Well, this strategy is somewhat contradictory, but it's important to note that not all of these strategies are compatible with one another. Also, some involve more risk than others, and this one is risky. So, what do we mean with "room to grow"?

Small market cap cryptocurrencies have more growth potential than the ones at the top. Of course, other factors will determine if the price will rise or not but the idea is that, if you invest in cryptocurrencies before they are big, you may get to see your investment grow several times over.

Now, before you go to the nearest exchange and start stacking up on useless meme coins, have a think about what you want to buy. Then, perform your due diligence, check the roadmap, check the team, read the whitepaper, learn about the technology. Do everything in your power to ensure that your investment is justified. This will also make it easier for you to stick to your strategy, knowing that you are invested in something you believe in.

TECHNICAL ANALYSIS

Yes, chart wizardry. To be honest, I have no idea how it works and I admire anyone that does. All those numbers and lines give me headaches. Nevertheless, if you have it in you, learning T.A. can do wonders for your investment strategy even if you only touch the surface! We asked Jonathan Hobbs, CFA and author of the Stop Saving Start Investing: Ten Simple Rules for Effectively Investing in Funds investment book how technical analysis can be useful even for a newbie investor. He stated:

"Any good investment strategy needs rules. Technical Analysis (or "TA") uses rules to look for price and volume patterns in charts to try and predict what's going to happen next. It helps investors choose when to buy or sell. One example of TA is the Simple Moving Average (or "SMA"). The 50-day SMA, for instance, is the average price over the last 50 days, which changes or 'moves' each day. When an investment starts trading above its SMA, this is could be a bullish sign. Since TA can also protect the downside, it's a good risk management tool for volatile investments like cryptocurrencies."

PROOF OF STAKE INTEREST

A lot of people would love to invest in cryptocurrency mining, but at this point, you either go big or go home. Mining has become an industrialized practice reserved only for those with large financial backing, high tech equipment and access to low energy prices. Although there are several alternatives to traditional mining, Proof of Stake is the most relevant one for the subject at hand.

To put it simply, Proof of Stake allows users to "mine" coins without mining equipment. In this system, the amount of coins a user holds will determine how many coins he mines. Although most PoS cryptocurrencies will require you to leave your wallet running, some implementations of PoS like Waves and Lisk allow you to earn interest by leasing or delegating your stake.

Do note that you shouldn't go out and buy every PoS coin out there. You should, however, check your holdings for these types of coins and, if you have them, mine them! In the worst case scenario, you'll need to leave the wallet running which can be done with any laptop or even a Raspberry Pi device.

The Security of Bitcoin

Not only has Bitcoin's value gone up over the past year, but the available options for Bitcoin storage have also increased. The choice can be especially intimidating for Bitcoin novices.

No matter what you choose, however, there is always a tradeoff between convenience and security. And while privacy is also a factor, here we assume you are not willing to go the extra step of anonymizing and completely eradicating your financial trail.

(Those interested in how to use Bitcoin with full anonymity, look at ExpressVPN's guide to Bitcoin anonymity, which includes a step-by-step tutorial.)

Classifications of Bitcoin Transactions

Bitcoin usage can be separated into two independent variables: "Transaction volume" and "Transaction value." Whether these values are high are low changes which Bitcoin wallet is best for you.

"Transaction volume" is the rate of bitcoin transactions you make. This might mean one transaction per day or only one per week. What counts as high or low in this case is fairly arbitrary.

"Transaction value" is the bitcoin value of a given transaction. What defines a large bitcoin value is similarly ambiguous. A good rule of thumb is that a low transaction value is less than or equal to the amount of money you would be comfortable carrying around as cash in your pocket. Everything larger than that might be high value.

Multiple Bitcoin wallets might be the best solution for you

There is absolutely no need for you to restrict yourself to a simple solution. Maybe the way you use Bitcoin includes all the use cases listed below, such as regular small payments, regular large payments, and long-term investments.

Use multiple options in parallel to make the most out of keeping Bitcoins both accessible and secure.

FIND THE BITCOIN SOLUTION FOR YOU

	Few transactions	Many transactions
Small value	Online Wallet	Mobile Wallet
Large value	Paper Wallet	Hardware Wallet

IF YOU MAKE MANY TRANSACTIONS OF LOW VALUE

Mobile Wallet

If you are making a lot of transactions with low value (e.g., because you mostly use Bitcoin to buy socks, tea, or a VPN), then you should use a mobile wallet that you control the keys to.

With a mobile wallet, your Bitcoins are always accessible as long as your phone has power. If you use a modern smartphone with an up-to-date operating system, your Bitcoins are secure. Don't forget to back up your seed phrase on a piece of paper and store that paper somewhere securely! Have a look at our recommendations for Android and iOS Bitcoin wallets.

IF YOU MAKE MANY TRANSACTIONS OF HIGH VALUE

Hardware Wallet

If a lot of money is at stake, like if you conduct a business that deals with Bitcoin a lot, or because you pay some of your staff in cryptocurrency, then you need a hardware wallet. Hardware wallets look like USB sticks and store your Bitcoin private keys on a specialized chip, similar to the secure enclave in an iPhone.

Even if your phone or computer were to get hacked, your hardware wallet would be unaffected. Since the wallet is password protected, someone who steals or finds your wallet would not be able to access it.

Unlike all other options, hardware wallets cost money, ranging from €29 for the cheapest Ledger Wallet, to $99 USD for the Trezor, which also acts as a FIDO U2F key.

As with other wallets, you should store a backup of your seed on a piece of paper somewhere and keep it in a safe place. That way, if you lose your hardware wallet, you don't lose your Bitcoins.

IF YOU MAKE FEW TRANSACTIONS OF HIGH VALUE

Paper Wallet

If you have significant savings in Bitcoin that you do not need to spend or more frequently, then a paper wallet is best for you. Don't use an online service to create your paper wallet, but rather create one yourself.

The most secure option is to get yourself a copy of the operating system TAILS, which comes with the Bitcoin wallet Electrum installed. Crawl under a blanket or tent, boot it up and create a Bitcoin wallet. You write down the seed on a piece of paper and shut down the computer.

As TAILS by default keeps no data on your USB stick and wipes the internal RAM, there are no traces of your seed left on the computer. As long as you can secure the paper, your Bitcoins are secure. Have a look at ExpressVPN's Bitcoin security tips!

To send your Bitcoins, you will have to again boot into a TAILS instance and restore a wallet using the seed from your paper.

IF YOU MAKE FEW TRANSACTIONS OF LOW VALUE

Online Wallet

If you only keep a small amount of Bitcoin and rarely spend them, have a look at an online wallet service, like Blockchain.info (they also have an onion site!).

Unlike with your mobile wallet, you will not have to worry what happens when you switch devices. You can log into your account using an email address and a password. When you sign up, carefully go through the security options to lock down your account from hackers while keeping it accessible to you. Using a strong password and a password manager is a good idea!

Many Bitcoin wallets for many uses

There are many ways to use Bitcoin and as many ways to keep them. Be aware of what you want to use your Bitcoins for, and how accessible they need to be. There is often a trade-off between accessibility and security, but by spreading your Bitcoins across different wallets, you can find the optimal situation!

CHAPTER 11:

AWESOME FACTS ABOUT BITCOIN

Here are ten awesome Bitcoin facts, success or disasters that you may not be aware of, enjoy!

BITCOIN STUDIES

You suddenly wish you could go back to university, but you only have bitcoins left because of your forward-thinking state of mind? Do not panic: you are now able to pay your tuition fees with Bitcoins for the famous New-Yorker university of The King's College!

However, if you are not living on the American soil, be aware that it exists the same kind of initiative, for example by the University of Cumbria in the United Kingdom, or also by the University of Nicosia, in Cyprus. The latter also features a degree in « Digital Currencies »for its student that highlights Bitcoin.

BITCOIN BOULEVARD

Are you visiting the Netherlands? Do not miss the Bitcoin Boulevard located in the Hague, which offers a unique feature: A high majority of shopkeepers who are located on the two streets that go alongside the channel – Bierkade and Groenewegje – now accept Bitcoin, following an initiative submitted by Hendrik Jan Hilbolling and Peter Klasen.

You can therefore have dinner in one of the nine restaurants that participate in the operation, or you can go shopping in the art gallery also located there, thanks to your favorite cryptocurrency. Some other streets seem to follow the same move, in particular in the United States: for example, the North-American Bitcoin Boulevard located in Cleveland Heights, in Ohio.

THE FIRST TRANSACTION

Bitcoin has enabled 43 472 379 transactions since its creation through its network. However, you will be certainly interested in knowing who initiated the first transaction.

It is no one else but Satoshi Nakamoto, the fantastic Bitcoin and underlying technology creator, who sent 100 bitcoins to Hal Finney on January 12th, 2009.

Hal Finney has been involved for a long time in the cryptography community. For years, he has been working with PGP Corporation, developing one of the most famous encryption system (The company was holding the rights for the PGP system, developed at the origin by Phil Zimmermann). He launched then the first anonymous remailer used to encode his emails and was also implicated in the cypher-punks' movement.

On a Bitcointalks post, Hal explained how it happened:

When Satoshi announced the first release of the software, I grabbed it right away. I think I was the first person besides Satoshi to run Bitcoin [client]. I mined block 70-something, and I was the recipient of the first Bitcoin transaction, when

Satoshi sent ten coins to me as a test. I carried on an email conversation with Satoshi over the next few days, mostly me reporting bugs and him fixing them.

After a few days, Bitcoin [client] was running pretty stably, so I left it running. Those were the days when difficulty was 1, and you could find blocks with a CPU, not even a GPU. I mined several blocks over the next days. But I turned it off because it made my computer run hot, and the fan noise bothered me. In retrospect, I wish I had kept it up longer, but on the other hand, I was extraordinarily lucky to be there, at the beginning. It's one of those glass half full half empty things.

THE MILLION DOLLAR BITCOIN

PIZZA

On May 22nd, 2010, a Bitcoiner named Laszlo Hanyecz paid to a Bitcointalks forum user not less than 10 000 BTC for two Papa John's pizzas. What can be considered as an incredible amount (5 619 700$ worth of BTC nowadays) was equivalent to 30$, according to the exchange rate applied at this time, estimated to 0,003 cents per Bitcoin. Mr. Hanyecz said he had acquired these bitcoins by mining on his computer.

"It wasn't like bitcoins had any value back then, so the idea of trading them for pizza was incredibly cool," said Mr. Hanyecz. But when asked about the current value of the cryptocurrency, he adds: "No one knew it was going to get so big."

Questioned about possible regrets, he adds:

"No, not really," Mr. Hanyecz said. Then he sold his bitcoins when the price was around 1$, getting 4000$ "That was enough to get a new computer and a couple of new video cards, so I'd say I ended up on top."

A BITCOIN MASTER SWINDLE

On November 4th, 2011, a BitcoinTalks forum user named pirateat40 has announced the creation of a Bitcoin investment fund, promising to the investors a return on investment of 7% per week.

Despite numerous suspicious elements and ridiculous incentives to invest such as "It's growing, it's growing!", "I have yet to come close to taking a loss on any deal," and even "risk is almost 0", the fund encountered a fast and great success: according to the SEC report, more than 700 467 BTC, the equivalent of 411,7 million dollars, have been collected by Trendon Shavers, a.k.a pirateat40.

Contrary to the presentations made to the investors, the fund was not performing any trading activities; in addition, the users have never seen their « invested » bitcoins again.

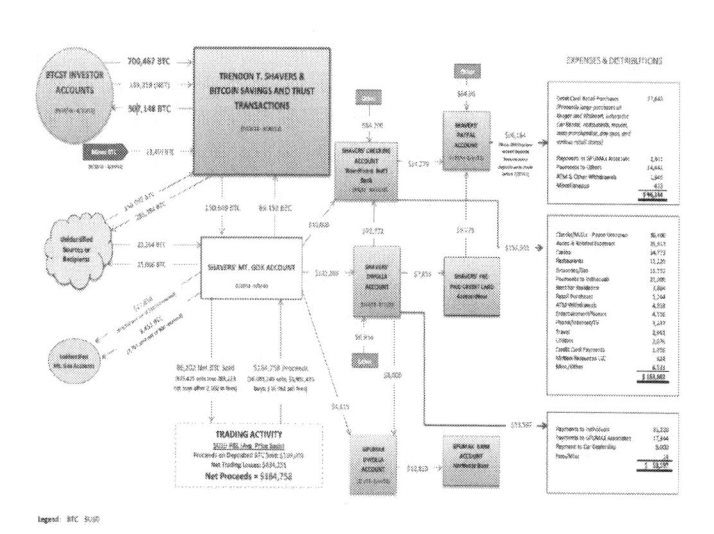

Here is an infographic explaining the whole swindle scheme

MORE BITCOIN USERS IN POLAND THAN IN FRANCE

While France is way ahead in terms of GDP (2,737,361 Millions of USD, FMI, 2013) at the 5th position, and Poland is at the 22nd position (516,128 Millions of USD, FMI, 2013), it seems that there are more Bitcoin users in Poland than in France!

This is the stunning fact that the download statistics of the most-downloaded Bitcoin client (Bitcoin-Core, totalizing 5M+ downloads) seem to indicate since January 2009: it has been downloaded 124,748 times by users having an IP located in Poland since January 2009, against 106,780 in France.

A first sketch of the explanation can be found in the progressive state of mind adopted by the Polish government:

Everything that is not forbidden is allowed. However, in light of EU legislation, we can't recognize Bitcoin as legal tender or electronic money. Bitcoin capital gains are taxed as ordinary income. [...] We don't stand in the way of bitcoin's development, but we need a declaration from its users whether they expect any regulations to be introduced or rather prefer the government to stand aside.

Krzysztof Piech, Ph.D. from Warsaw School of Economics, said that Poland is in the top 10 in the number of bitcoins mined, and Polish bitcoin trading volume is one of the biggest in the world. He also emphasized bitcoin's potential for the Polish economy.

However, to reassure our French readers, we want to add that in terms of Bitcoin nodes, one has to admit that France keeps a clear advantage.

64% IS THE ESTIMATED PART OF PRESENT « GHOST » BITCOINS ON THE BLOCKCHAIN

..According to a study made by the California University

The history of Bitcoin is regularly studded by stories of users who have lost their private keys and who are not still able to use their bitcoins. See two examples of bitcoins who have not been spent for a very (very!) long while:

- 1FeexV6bAHb8ybZjqQMjJrcCrHGW9sb6uF : 75,957 bitcoins which have never been spent. Address created on March 1st 2011.

- 12tkqA9xSoowkzoERHMWNKsTey55YEBqkv : 28,150 bitcoins which have never been spent. Address created on April 5th, 2010.

THE COMPUTING POWER OF THE BITCOIN NETWORK IS 7468 TIMES HIGHER THAN THE ONE OF THE

CUMULATIVE 500 WORLD

SUPERCOMPUTERS

Indeed, the computing power of the whole Bitcoin network is estimated to 2 046 364 Pflop/s, against 274 Pflop/s for the cumulative 500 most powerful world supercomputers.

First of all, it is important to note that Bitcoin miners are not performing any floating point operations (FLOP) but only integer calculus. How have we then been able to proceed? It's very easy, in fact:

1 hash = 6.35K integer operations

1 integer operation = 2 floating point operations

1 hash = 12.7K floating point operations

Then, using this rate of one hash = 12,7K flop, and by analyzing the current hashrate of the Bitcoin network which peaks to 161 131 086 gh/s on July 31st, 2014, we get an estimation of $10^9*161131086$ H/s * 12700 = 2 046 364,7922 Petaflops.

So much computing power that could have been possibly used in modelization purposes, for medicine, astronomy, physics. Damn bitcoiners!

THE LARGEST TRANSACTION EVER MADE ON THE NETWORK: 194 993 BTC

https://blockchain.info/tx/1c12443203a48f42cdf7b1acee5b4b1c1fedc144cb909a3bf5edbffafb0cd204

It represents more than 114 million of dollars, according to the effective rate on 07/31/2014. « A shitload of money » is the comment submitted by the recipient of the funds about the transaction. We can only agree!

Some Reddit users, such as gen_gen, had fun by trying to identify the author of this colossal transaction :

Interesting findings:

Going further down the tree from that tx shows that these two addresses are extremely likely Bitstamp cold wallets:

17ewBhK712mY2E4uPAbinThibdY2LRyabd (85,993 BTC)

1DKH2oZtrcAAoZXsNJQnKBwKYaYdx5KrVV (39,200 BTC)

Also based on *https://blockchain.info/tx/5d8a61b66c003743ba782b0b 3931a782d8e0f1cdd8e4c2551faf15fc9334bdb5, it looks like 1Drt3c8pSdrkyjuBiwVcSSixZwQtMZ3Tew is a Bitstamp hot wallet.*

And gen_gen was right!

BITCOIN'S TIGER WOODS

In October 2009, so more than 10 months after the launch of the cryptocurrency, the bitcoins were traded at an extremely competitive rate: 1$ for 1,309BTC which is equivalent to less than 0,00076$ per Bitcoin.

Assuming you had spent 308 dollars in order to acquire your first 403,712 bitcoins, and that you would have sold them in December 2013 at the famous peak of $1240 / BTC, you would have a fortune of $501,556,440, which is the personal wealth of Tiger Woods added of one million of dollars ($500 000 000)!

Not a golf fan? No problem, let's focus on soccer. You would have had to spend 80$ in bitcoins (104,720 BTC) in order to overtake the fortune of the international star Christiano Ronaldo, namely $130,000,000.

CHAPTER 12:

CRYPTOCURRENCY MARKET MOVING BEYOND BITCOIN?

More than a currency exchange. More than a simple coin. This is the power of Ethereum.

There is no way you've missed seeing Ethereum mentioned if you've been involved in any way with cryptocurrencies. And with good reason.

Ethereum began out of a need to see bitcoin's underlying technology – the blockchain – used for something greater than simply sending currency from one user to another. Vitalik, the creator of Ethereum, built the system to be a "world computer" incorporating a virtual machine (EVM), a Turing-complete language (Solidity, Viper), a token (ETH), and fuel (gas).

WHAT IS ETHEREUM?

Ether, traded under the code ETH, can be purchased at exchanges and used to pay for products and services at most merchants that accept cryptocurrencies. After all, it's the second biggest cryptocurrency by market cap at the time of writing.

Ether is also used to pay for transaction fees and for computational services when using the Ethereum network.

Ether is mined similarly to bitcoin, ie, you set your computer to attempt to solve the question present on a particular block in the blockchain. Once you find the answer, you get paid in ETH.

However, the goal of Ethereum is to be something greater than a coin. Not happy with how the blockchain technology was being underutilized by bitcoin, the creators of Ethereum set out to truly take the blockchain to the next level. They envisage a method to decentralize the Internet itself.

WHY A DECENTRALIZED SYSTEM?

To understand what a decentralized system is, you need to understand how our current networking systems work, ie, centralized systems. Let's say you have an online account where you store photos. Let's call it "CloudPhoto". You can upload photos to CloudPhoto, and you can access those photos from anywhere. Now let's say something goes wrong, and CloudPhoto's servers burn down. Unfortunately, you can't access your photos, and all are lost.

This is a centralized system. Usually, we mitigate this scenario by creating backups of our data, making copies of the same data and storing them elsewhere or by keeping different groups of data on different servers. This decentralizes the system.

Decentralisation is also beneficial in cases where you need to maintain the integrity of data. For example, keeping all the student grades at a school on one computer is a problem because if someone hacks into that computer and changes those grades, then there would be no way to catch the change. If ten different computers held onto the student scores, it would be easy to recognize that one of the computers holding the data is wrong and consequently fix that data set.

So a decentralized system is one where there is no single point of failure. This has many obvious advantages, and you need to keep that in mind when considering Ethereum.

ETHEREUM VIRTUAL MACHINE AND DAPPS

Decentralised Applications, or DApps, is the driving force behind Ethereum's development, and they run on the Ethereum virtual machine, also known as the World Computer. This virtual machine is Ethereum's defining development and it allows applications to run on the blockchain.

As discussed in the "Why a decentralized system?" section, centralized systems suffer from single points of failures. If something were to happen to eBay, and they didn't have any backups, you would lose all evidence of your hard-earned success. Decentralised Apps run on the blockchain and make use of it to maintain data scattered across all users of Ethereum. The data sets are, of course, encrypted so as to not be accessible by everyone, but everyone would be able to verify and validate the data if the need arises.

There are already many DApps, from online gambling to prediction markets and social media platforms, and most likely there are many more to come.

THE DAO HACK

Smart contracts are the basis of the Ethereum ecosystem and platform: someone creates a contract with rules and triggers, and the smart contract executes when the trigger event occurs, as long as all the rules can be enforced.

The Decentralised Autonomous Organisation, or DAO, was to be the crown jewel of the Ethereum smart contract and virtual machine ecosystem: a smart contract that was going to build a decentralized venture capital fund with the aim of providing funding for all future DApp development. People would invest into the DAO, and they would be allowed to vote on which DApps got funding, and which did not.

The DAO launched on 30 April 2016 and within 28 days, it had accumulated more than US$150 million worth of ETH. The attack happened on 17 June 2016 and it worked by exploiting a loophole in the way investors left the DAO. If you wanted to leave the DAO (as an investor), you were allowed to take all the ETH you had invested after you returned the DAO tokens you had been given when investing (a sort of stakeholder system).

The problem was that the contract had two steps, as outlined above:

1. Take DAO tokens from user, and give back ETH from DAO to user.

2. Register the transaction in the blockchain and update the DAO token count.

The hack was simple in hindsight: inject a step between step 1 and step 2 above where, before the transaction gets registered, the DAO would give the same user more ETH for the same tokens.

This hack cost the DAO US$50 million worth of ETH and caused the value of ETH to plummet from US$20.17 to US$11.52 in 48 hours.

Ethereum Classic

Ethereum Classic, ETC, is a fork of Ethereum, ETH, which came about as a result of the way the developers and community behind Ethereum decide to handle the DAO attack.

After the DAO attack, the Ethereum community agreed that the best course of action was to hold the money taken by the hacker and return everything to the people who invested in the DAO, practically rewinding the hacker's attack. Many Ethereum users did not agree with this as, in their opinion, it went against the core philosophy of cryptocurrencies: the blockchain is immutable and should not be affected by the whims of its users.

Reverting the attack and forking the code to reset the blockchain went against the core philosophy that the code is law, and so many people stayed with the original blockchain, Ethereum Classic.

WHERE CAN I USE ETH?

ETH has been on the rise since its inception and has been enjoying widespread acceptance by investors, exchanges and merchants. At the time of writing this, in September 2017, websites using cart software like WooCommerce and OpenCart can be set up to accept ETH payments and we will likely be seeing even more merchants popping up online that accept ETH.

But currently, in September 2017, the biggest use for ETH is as a stake in Ethereum, an investment in the smart contract platform of the future. Perhaps that future will include a completely decentralized Internet where the centralized system of DNS and servers has become obsolete, returning power to the users themselves.

How do I invest in Ethereum?

There are many ways to invest in Ethereum, the simplest of which is to buy some ETH and hold it. As more users buy ETH, more merchants will likely see the value of accepting ETH as payment, which may increase the value of the coin. An increase in the value of the coin would give more strength to the developers behind the Ethereum network and the DApps running on it, and this would in turn increase the value of your held assets.

As can be seen here, ETH went from US$12.836/ETH in February 2017...

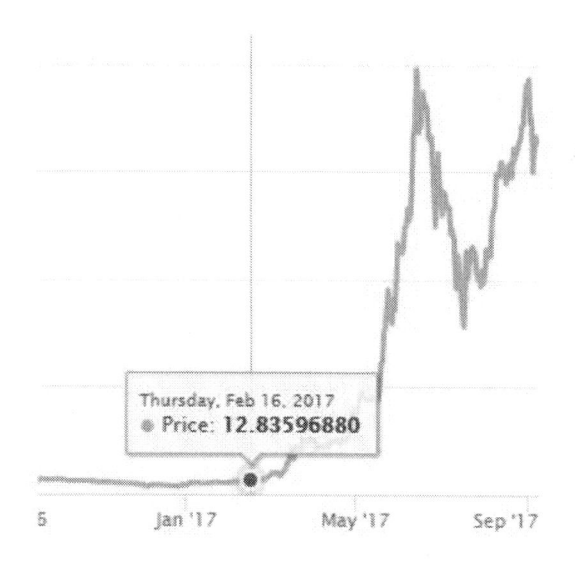

... to US$343.949 in just 4 months!

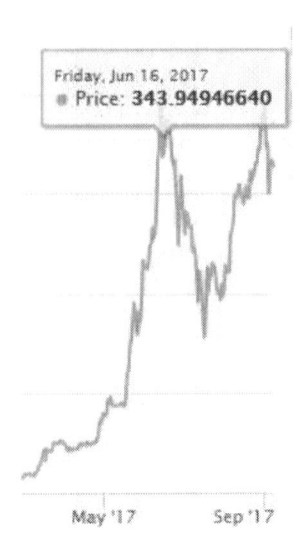

Friday, Jun 16, 2017
Price: 343.94946640

That's an incredible growth, and while the coin is currently struggling to break the resistance at US$380-390 (September 2017), if it does eventually break it, there's no telling where it might go.

HOW TO TRANSFER MONEY WITH ETHEREUM

Transferring ETH works just as it would work with any other cryptocurrency:

1. Have some ETH in your wallet. The official Ethereum wallet can be download either from GitHub or from the official website.

2. Scan or enter the recipient's address. Whether they provide you with the hashed wallet address or a QR code, just follow the simple instructions on your wallet of choice and you'll be done in no time.

3. Enter the amount and send. The transaction should be verified in a few seconds and you're done.

Making money with Ethereum

• Get paid in ETH. Adopting ETH as tender for your products or services is the simplest and most effective way of making money with a cryptocurrency like Ethereum. If you're a writer, designer, artist or developer, you can ask to be paid in ETH. If you're selling clothes, vape products, posters or DVDs, you can ask to be paid in ETH. Every sale affected with

ETH helps Ethereum grow and as it grows so does the value of that same ETH sitting in your wallet.

• Invest in Ethereum. If you're willing to shell out some USD (or fiat currency of your choice), you can buy the ETH directly at an exchange and hold it. More people holding ETH in their wallet could instill confidence in the currency and as confidence increases so does the value of the coin. If you had bought $1,000 worth of ETH in January 2017, in June you would have owned US$26,795 instead.

WHAT TO WATCH OUT FOR

Ethereum is trying to be bigger and better than simple currencies like bitcoin, but the huge advantages it offers might also be its downfall.

• Never just a coin. Ethereum wants to be something more than a cryptocurrency and this might cause problems. A platform is harder to maintain, harder to develop and harder to see adoption. A cryptocurrency is simple: buy and sell things using that currency.

Bitcoin, for example, is nothing more than a currency and people, especially businesses and merchants, like simple things that just work.

• Big things in the future. With a roadmap as ambitious as Ethereum's, the road is bound to be a little rocky. After all, platforms have failed for introducing far smaller, and far simpler new features that had unforeseen, fatal side-effects. This is obviously not a certainty, but it's good to be mindful of big changes coming in the future of Ethereum.

WHAT'S NEXT FOR ETHEREUM?

Ethereum's roadmap is sprawling and ambitious. Apart from a strong drive to have ETH accepted by more merchants there are some promising things in Ethereum's future.

• More DApps. Ethereum is a platform for building decentralized apps. From smart contracts to crowdfunding projects to autonomous organizations, just as a computer is only as effective as the software written for it, Ethereum is only as successful as the DApps running on it. This is definitely an exciting time for everyone from simple users of Ethereum to investors, developers and the cryptocurrency community as a whole.

• Proof-of-Stake. Similar to the Proof-of-Importance system used on NEM, Ethereum is working on shifting from a Proof-of-Work (POW) mining method to a Proof-of-Stake (POS) generation of ETH instead.

POW is a system in which your computer works hard at some puzzle or other that helps maintain the integrity of the Ethereum platform, and your wallet is rewarded with some amount of ETH for your efforts.

POS works by having a user lock up a percentage of their ETH assets in order to verify a segment of transactions on the Ethereum network, from which the user would receive ETH (possibly as part of the transaction fees paid in every transaction). This is considered a fairer system than POW as it relies on the user having a stake in the platform instead of being able to purchase a strong computer that runs more computations than someone else's.

Ripple

The fast money transfer network, Ripple, and its associated coin, XRP, have been enjoying steady acceptance and growth over the five years since their inception. Here's why.

When talking about Ripple (XRP), people often overlook the product that caused it to exist: the Ripple Network. Unfortunately, even though it's been accepted by several banks as a legitimate money transfer system, the platform is a bit more complex to figure out than your regular cryptocurrency.

So we're going to go through it and explain every piece along the way.

What is Ripple?

The goal of Ripple is to be a global settlement network, a platform to allow anyone to transfer money in any currency to any currency in a matter of seconds. This is an ambitious goal meant to eliminate the use of older systems like Western Union or SWIFT.

The alternative Ripple proposes is the use of XRP as a common currency underlying all money transfers between different currencies (USD is currently the most common currency). Not only are transaction fees much lower to convert from one currency to XRP and back, but transfers take a maximum of 4 seconds to execute and verify.

Quite a few global banks have already started embracing Ripple as it saves them a lot of money in the long run by avoiding exchange fees.

How is Ripple different from Bitcoin?

The Ripple coin and the Ripple Network have various advantages over bitcoin as they have been built with slightly different purposes in mind.

Fast and cheap

Ripple transaction processing only takes four seconds since it's significantly less active compared to bitcoin. This has the added bonus of cheaper transaction fees, whereas the price for bitcoin transactions has been on the rise lately as more people adopt the platform.

Mining-free

All the 100 billion XRP that it's possible to use on the platform already exist. While they're not all on the market — a few are released into the market every month to avoid flooding — there is no use mining as there is nothing of value to be added, unlike in more traditional cryptocurrencies.

Bank acceptance

The Ripple platform and coin being accepted by banks gives the process legitimacy and, at least from an investor's standpoint, can be a little more reassuring. This is not the case with bitcoin and other currencies as they are seen as competition by the banks.

WHERE CAN I USE RIPPLE?

XRP is still a long way from being as widely accepted as coins such as Bitcoin, Litecoin or Ethereum. It was never the goal to use Ripple as a payment method. Instead, the aim has always been to use XRP to grease the wheels, in order to make fiat money transfers easier, faster and more secure.

That said, there are quite a few merchants that accept Ripple, including hosting providers and vaping product merchants. A full list can be found on the XRP forum here.

HOW DO I INVEST IN RIPPLE?

Rarely has a coin been considered so ripe for purchase as Ripple is in September, 2017. Selling at $0.0218 per XRP on 1 April 2017...

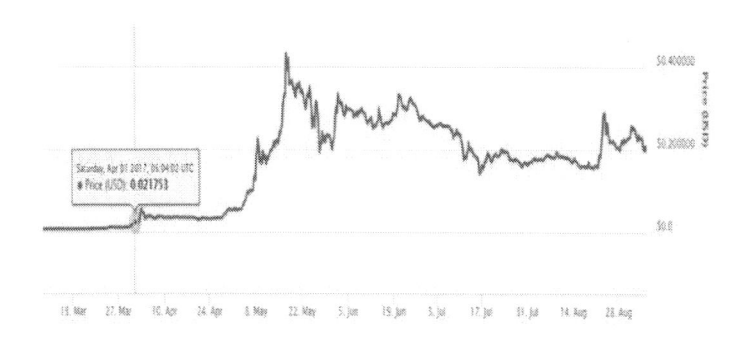

...the coin skyrocketed to $0.3973 per XRP in no more than 47 days!

The price has since settled down a bit as speculators decide whether they want to invest in the coin or not, and banks shuffle funds around and investigate the platform.

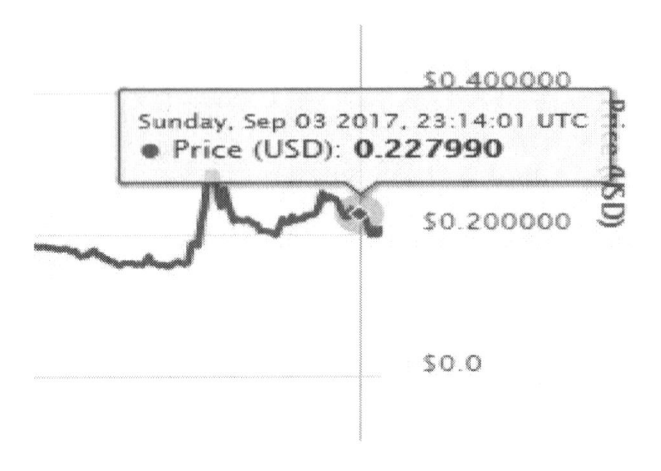

```
                                    $0.400000
         Sunday, Sep 03 2017, 23:14:01 UTC
         ● Price (USD): 0.227990

                                    $0.200000


                                    $0.0
```

With more bank involvement will come greater growth. If you have no problem with the way Ripple has handled the initial XRP influx (see section below: "What to watch out for – Centralisation) and if you think more banks will accept Ripple as the de facto money transfer platform, then there may never be a better time to get in on Ripple than 2017.

Using Ripple to transfer money

Transferring money with Ripple works like any other cryptocurrency:

1. Have some XRP available in your wallet. XRP wallets are the same as, for example, bitcoin wallets. Buy XRP on an exchange and then transfer them to your wallet.

2. Scan or enter the recipient's address. Whether they provide you with the hashed wallet address or a QR code, just follow the simple instructions on your wallet of choice and you'll be done in no time.

3. Enter the amount and send. The transaction should be verified in a few seconds and you're done.

Making money with Ripple

Unless you're a bank willing to invest into the Ripple platform, and because there is no mining allowed on

Ripple, there are only two major ways to make money from it.

GET PAID IN RIPPLE

Adopting XRP will not only put you in a position where you can see returns on money that's sitting in your wallet, but you will also be helping the currency gain legitimacy and wider use. Being this early and this young, Ripple will benefit from any merchant accepting the currency. When it grows, everyone enjoys the fruits of their investment.

INVEST IN RIPPLE

While the Ripple platform might not be easily accessible for investors, anyone can buy XRP and wait. The currency is growing and it is still in its infant stage. As more and more merchants and banks adopt the platform, the price will probably increase, the currency will grow and the value of every wallet will grow with it.

WHAT TO WATCH OUT FOR

As much as some people love Ripple and see it as the next generation of cryptocurrencies, there are also some who have concerns over privacy and centralization.

• *Privacy concerns*

Cryptocurrency has always been considered the poster child of privacy and anonymity. Ripple's decision to market their platform exclusively to banks has been a cause of concern for some users who worry about big brother keeping an eye on their transactions.

• *Centralisation*

Ripple's platform is extremely centralized whereas most cryptocurrencies aim to be as decentralized as possible. The reason for this is that Ripple owns the vast majority of the coins available on the platform while currencies like bitcoin allow anyone to mine and acquire coins. The move to lock coins inside smart contracts was a step in the right direction to fix this issue, but every time the coins are released they first go to Ripple to do with them as it pleases.

WHAT'S NEXT FOR RIPPLE?

The company behind Ripple plans, as a priority, to improve the lack of decentralization from which the platform is currently suffering. By adding more trusted validator nodes, the company plans to shake off the image that it's just another central bank controlling the Ripple currency.

With that said, the future of Ripple depends entirely on the adoption of the platform by banks and that's where the focus of the people behind Ripple inevitably needs to be. As more banks join the network, the price of XRP will probably skyrocket, driving more people to the coin and enticing banks to join the platform.

Without banks the platform would likely die, and so will the investors attempting to push it forward. Luckily, that doesn't seem to be the future of this currency.

LITECOIN

Faster and more secure than Bitcoin, Litecoin has been enjoying explosive growth in 2017. Let's take a closer look at why.

Having started from very modest origins and possessing only subtle technical improvements over bitcoin, Litecoin has grown to become the second largest cryptocurrency on the market. It is now often characterized as the silver to bitcoin's gold, but there's far more to the currency's sudden growth than meets the eye.

What is Litecoin?

Released on 7 October 2011 by former Google employee Charlie Lee, Litecoin (LTC, Ł) is an open source, peer-to-peer cryptocurrency – digital currency operating independently of any country's central bank. While similar to bitcoin in many ways, Litecoin also incorporates several improvements (such as Segregated Witness) which help reduce bottlenecks in the network and increase the speed with which transactions are carried out.

Litecoin has experienced massive growth since its inception, reaching a $1 billion market cap in November 2013, and over four times that much by 2017.

How is Litecoin different from Bitcoin?

While there are a lot of similarities between Litecoin and its more widely accepted competitor, bitcoin,

Litecoin has a few distinct advantages when it comes to mining, transaction verification speed, and security:

• Higher volume of transactions. The Segregated Witness process increases the rate at which transactions are verified on the block, reducing the time for confirmation of payment from 10 minutes (for bitcoin) to 2.5 minutes (for Litecoin).

• More secure. This faster processing time also helps maintain a secure environment by reducing the chance of double-spending attacks – a hack in which the attacker spends the same money twice to pay for two different transactions.

• Larger coin limit. While bitcoin has a maximum coin limit of 21 million coins, Litecoin has an upper limit of 84 million coins.

• Harder to mine. This might not be seen as an advantage at first glance, but because Litecoin uses script hashing (instead of SHA-256) mining cannot be accelerated by using parallel processors, as can be done when bitcoin mining. This has created a much more level playing field as opposed to the arms race that bitcoin mining has become.

Where can I use Litecoin?

You can use Litecoin nearly anywhere you can use bitcoin. Since its release, it has become the second largest cryptocurrency after bitcoin, and merchants have been quick to adopt it. The Litecoin website has an always-growing list of services, merchants and providers that accept Litecoin, ranging from financial consulting services to health and beauty product merchants.

How do I invest in Litecoin?

As with most other cryptocurrencies, there are quite a few ways to put some Litecoin in your wallet.

• Purchase directly from an exchange. The easiest and most straightforward method of acquiring Litecoin is to buy some from an exchange. Exchanges mostly accept credit card payments, cheques, and some even money transfers, and will in turn deposit Litecoin into your wallet. Exchanges also usually charge a percentage fee for their service, typically in the 0.5-2% range, depending on the service provider and the volume of Litecoin you're exchanging.

• Receive payment in Litecoin. Whether you're providing a service or selling goods to a consumer, you can always accept Litecoin as payment just as you would any other currency. With its lower fees, commissions and costs, compared to receiving fiat money (ie, government-issued currency), receiving payment in Litecoin results in more money in your pocket. Additionally, Litecoin transactions are secure, faster and less susceptible to fraud.

• Earn Litecoin through mining. Generating Litecoin through the process known as mining is slow and requires specialized equipment to be worth the effort, but it is nonetheless a legitimate method of generating coins. You can just put your computer to work, validating and verifying transactions made on the Litecoin network by other users, and in return, you are paid in Litecoin. The faster you can mine, the more Litecoin you can make.

Using Litecoin to Transfer Money

As with cryptocurrencies in general, payments with Litecoin are lightning fast and incredibly easy. To pay someone with Litecoin:

1. Enter the person's address into your wallet application, or scan the QR code that corresponds to that address.
2. Enter the amount of Litecoin you'd like to send.
3. Send.

That's it. There's nothing else to it.

Making money with Litecoin

Over the years, Litecoin has attracted a lot of speculators and currency investors looking to make money from the rise and fall of the cryptocurrency.

It's most explosive growth came in 2017, on the heels of Bitcoin's meteoric rise. Sitting at a measly $3.80/LTC March 01, 2017...

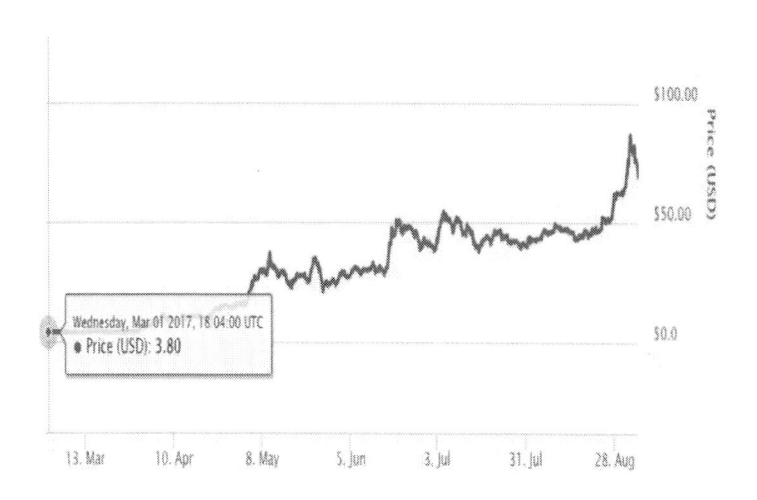

...it multiplied its value by an unprecedented 22x in just 6 months to reach a high of $84.09/LTC on September 01, 2017.

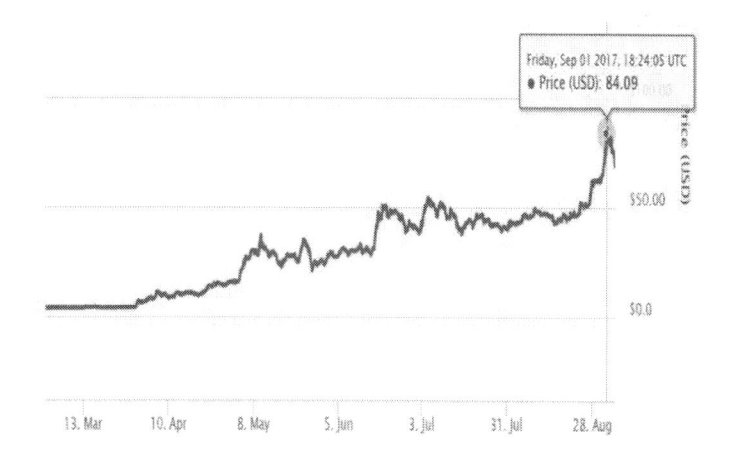

Because of its growing popularity and cost, many investors have taken to buying Litecoin and then reselling it when the price increases. This is a very popular strategy but it also comes with its own pitfalls. Litecoin prices are extremely volatile – quick rises often mean quick falls – and you should always be very careful and spend time studying the currency before making any costly investment decisions.

WHAT TO WATCH OUT FOR

Not unlike its bigger sibling, Litecoin has its disadvantages. Here are a few of the cryptocurrency's shortcomings:

• Not as widely accepted. Litecoin is still growing and while its acceptance has become more and more common, bitcoin is still the most commonly recognized cryptocurrency.

• Not different enough. Many consider Litecoin's technical improvements too subtle and this might hinder Litecoin's growth. Faster transaction times and more difficulty in mining might be good enough reasons for specific-use cases, but in the grand scheme of things, many are of the opinion that it does not differentiate itself from bitcoin enough to sustain long term growth.

THE FUTURE OF LITECOIN

Litecoin's market cap growth is not expected to slow down anytime soon which will lead to more and more businesses adopting the altcoin, either alongside bitcoin or as a complete replacement.

Additionally, a lot of work is being carried out on improving the network Litecoin runs on, which will improve the speed at which transactions are verified even further and will, more importantly, allow Atomic Swaps.

With new Litecoin ATMs being installed and a growing number of companies slowly making the switch to Litecoin, its future is looking brighter than ever.

CHAPTER 13:

THE SECRETS OF CRYPTOCURRENCY

There has been a lot of speculation around whether cryptocurrency is safe to use or whether it will be a bad investment. Recently a debut developed between cryptocurrency investors and the business giants of the world. Just like every other debut, it has two sides to the story, pro-cryptocurrency or against-cryptocurrency.

• Pro-cryptocurrency:

As you know, Cryptocurrency can be used for basically anything. This is how Lady Mone recently launched a major property development in Dubai. She believes that digital currency is a growing market that cannot be ignored.

Meanwhile, a property developer in London is allowing tenants to pay deposits in Bitcoin's.

Yann Quelenn, the analyst for Swissquote, says that cryptocurrency still holds great potential. He said that this could be a potential safe haven. Less than 0.01% of the world's population is in possession of a Bitcoin wallet. He believes that if this number is to reach 1%, the demand for bitcoin's would be through the roof, since there are only 18 million coins available.

In short, the pros for cryptocurrency are:

1. Cryptocurrency can be used to pay for anything.
2. It is a growing market with the potential for success.
3. The demand for digital money would skyrocket if the percentage of Bitcoin wallet holders reached 1%.

Looking at these pros, one might think that cryptocurrency will indeed make for a good investment; however, there are a few people out there who think cryptocurrency is just one big fraudulent scam.

• *Against-Cryptocurrency:*

According to Jamie Dimon, digital currency is only fit for drug dealers and murderers. He believes that Bitcoin is a scam that will blow up.

The boss of America's biggest bank said that this currency would not work. He said that people could not create a currency out of thin air. He also stated that he would immediately fire anyone who invests in cryptocurrency, as it is against their rules. And the person who invests in cryptocurrency is very stupid, and both of these are very dangerous.

Bitcoin emerged after a financial crisis. It allows you to bypass banks and traditional payment processes, creating a bigger risk of financial loss. Financial institutions are concerned about Bitcoin's association with money laundering and online crime.

After Dimon's comments, Bitcoin's value fell by 5%. He predicts anyone who is investing in this digital currency will for a fact lose their stakes.

In short, the cons are:

1. America's biggest bank does not believe cryptocurrency will be a success.

2. It bypasses banks and traditional ways of payment. Creating a bigger risk for financial loss.

3. It was previously associated with money laundering and online crime.

These arguments come from a very personal view on both sides. But will anybody ever be able to predict the outcome of a situation 100% to the mark? Cryptocurrency is new to the world and is at war with fiat money. Central banks are keen on preserving their monopoly on paper money and they will not give up without a fight.